Lett from Rising Pharmacy Stars

Advice on Creating and Advancing Your Career in a Changing Profession

SUSAN A. CANTRELL, RPh, CAE
Chief Executive Officer
Academy of Managed Care Pharmacy®
Alexandria, Virginia
And

SARA J. WHITE, RPh, MS, FASHP
Director of Pharmacy (ret.)
Stanford University Hospital and Clinics
Past President, ASHP
Palo Alto, California
Faculty
Pharmacy Leadership Academy and
leaders INNOVATION Master Series

Best wishes! Sm Cann

Any correspondence regarding this publication should be sent to the publisher, American Society of Health-System Pharmacists, 7272 Wisconsin Avenue, Bethesda, MD 20814, attention: Special Publishing.

The information presented herein reflects the opinions of the contributors and advisors. It should not be interpreted as an official policy of ASHP or as an endorsement of any product.

Because of ongoing research and improvements in technology, the information and its applications contained in this text are constantly evolving and are subject to the professional judgment and interpretation of the practitioner due to the uniqueness of a clinical situation. The editors and ASHP have made reasonable efforts to ensure the accuracy and appropriateness of the information presented in this document. However, any user of this information is advised that the editors and ASHP are not responsible for the continued currency of the information, for any errors or omissions, and/or for any consequences arising from the use of the information in the document in any and all practice settings. Any reader of this document is cautioned that ASHP makes no representation, guarantee, or warranty, express or implied, as to the accuracy and appropriateness of the information contained in this document and specifically disclaims any liability to any party for the accuracy and/or completeness of the material or for any damages arising out of the use or non-use of any of the information contained in this document.

Director, Special Publishing: Jack Bruggeman
Acquisitions Editor: Jack Bruggeman
Editorial Project Manager: Ruth Bloom
Production Manager: Johnna Hershey
Cover & Page Design: David Wade

Library of Congress Cataloging-in-Publication Data

Names: Cantrell, Susan A., compiler. | White, Sara J., 1945- compiler. |
    American Society of Health-System Pharmacists, issuing body.
Title: Letters from rising pharmacy stars : advice on creating and advancing
    your career in a changing profession / [edited by] Susan A. Cantrell and
    Sara J. White.
Description: Bethesda, MD : American Society of Health-System Pharmacists,
    [2017]
Identifiers: LCCN 2016045410 | ISBN 9781585285686
Subjects: | MESH: Pharmacists | Career Choice | Leadership | Job Satisfaction
    | United States | Personal Narratives | Collected Correspondence
Classification: LCC RS71 | NLM QV 21 | DDC 615.1092/2--dc23
LC record available at https://lccn.loc.gov/2016045410

Printed in Canada.

ISBN: 978-1-58528-568-6

10 9 8 7 6 5 4 3 2 1

Dedication

This book is dedicated to those pharmacists who selflessly give of their time serving as teachers, preceptors, residency directors, and mentors for the future leaders of our profession.

Acknowledgments

We are indebted to our many colleagues who contributed their time, life stories, and wisdom to this book. Our sincere appreciation also goes out to Jack Bruggeman, Ruth Bloom, and their colleagues in ASHP's Special Publishing Division for their vision, hard work, guidance, and patience throughout the development of this book.

Contents

★ Preface

Eleanor Roosevelt, former American first lady, diplomat, and activist, once famously said "The future belongs to those who believe in the beauty of their dreams." Those of us who are fortunate to be a part of the pharmacy community can attest to that statement. There are countless examples of pharmacists who, by believing in the beauty of their dreams, have blazed new trails, helped to reshape the profession, improved the lives of patients, and achieved extraordinary career successes. The stories of these accomplished pharmacy leaders are inspiring, and we believe that future or beginning pharmacists can learn a great deal from them.

Through mentorship of young and mid-career pharmacists, speaking to pharmacy residency classes, and serving as a preceptor to student pharmacists, we learned that young pharmacists have stories to share. We were inspired by many of these stories and realized, based on the success of the first *Letters* book, others might be as well. *Letters from Rising Pharmacy Stars* provides examples of young and mid-career pharmacy leaders faced with real-world issues and challenges— even some graduates of the "school of hard knocks"—and how they overcame and learned from their experiences.

One thing that was clear from the start, and became even clearer after we read the contributors' letters, was that the advice gleaned from these rising stars would be as compelling as the advice given by more seasoned pharmacists though quite different in perspectives and themes. The rising stars are, after all, still creating their stories and will have much more to tell. Likewise, they are practicing in a very different world of pharmacy than those who came before them. At the time of this writing, 38 states allow for some level of pharmacists' prescribing or modifying therapy under collaborative practice agreements with physicians, something that could barely be fathomed two decades ago. Most believe that pharmacists in the near future will receive provider status under the Centers for Medicare & Medicaid Services (CMS) regulations, something for which national pharmacy associations have diligently advocated. The world of pharmacy is in a period of rapid change, and these rising stars are not just living in it but are leading it.

The letters in this book describe how the words of famous people or the advice of mentors serve as a leadership moment, providing young pharmacists with courage and inspiration to follow paths less traveled in pharmacy practice. They offer advice on crafting your story, an important skill for new graduates and those seeking new career opportunities; navigating life and career as a two-pharmacist couple; becoming a pharmacist when both parents are pharmacists; developing a career as a pharmacogenetics clinical scientist; and dealing with the impact of significant life events such as a serious auto accident on your career and life. There are stories of how it is possible to have it all—family and successful careers. Letters also give insight into how to coordinate postgraduate year 1 and 2 (PGY1 and 2) residencies, what makes a good boss, and the irreplaceable value of mentors.

It is our hope that *Letters from Rising Pharmacy Stars* can shed light on some of the challenges and opportunities that might lie ahead and provide advice on how to handle them. The profession of pharmacy is a nurturing and close-knit community. Giving back to support those who come behind us is a well-regarded tradition in this great profession; it is in this spirit that we share these letters with our readers. We hope you will learn from others—both seasoned pharmacists and rising stars. To borrow the words of that great philosopher Yogi Berra, "You can observe a lot by just watching."

Susan A. Cantrell and Sara J. White
January 2017

Samm Anderegg, PharmD, MS, BCPS

Follow Your Passion, Focus on Relationships, Develop Expertise, and Enjoy the Ride

The influence and support of dedicated mentors opened Samm's eyes to opportunities he might not have known about otherwise, allowing him to develop unique and marketable skills. The more Samm encountered these willing mentors, the more comfortable he became seeking and accepting support. In his letter, he advises readers to do the same. Samm also sought to identify his strengths—and weaknesses—because he felt that self-awareness was the foundation of growth. His quest for self-awareness served him well and helped to make him a stronger team contributor.

Samm Anderegg is Project Manager and Consultant to the Pharmacy HIT (PHIT) Collaborative and is engaged in other contracts in the healthcare technology industry. Samm received his PharmD at the University of Iowa College of Pharmacy and a MS in Pharmacy Practice at the University of Kansas; he completed a postgraduate year (PGY) 1 and PGY2 residency at the University of Kansas Hospitals and College of Pharmacy. His work with the PHIT Collaborative focuses on providing an electronic framework for pharmacists to document patient care services in electronic systems.

Samm's advice is: **Experience, take risks, reflect, learn, and grow constantly. Eventually, you'll be the one doing the mentoring.**

Dear Young Pharmacist,

Your career in pharmacy will likely be long and rewarding. There are several lessons you will learn along the way. I'd like to share a few important experiences and how they have impacted my career. Mentorship, vulnerability, self-awareness, and hard work are consistent themes. Your goal is not to be perfect but to experience, learn, and grow throughout your career. *We rarely master things and are constantly "working on it."* Follow your passion, focus on relationships, develop expertise, and enjoy the ride.

During pharmacy school, one of our lectures covered the history of pharmacy and how we've evolved from chemists to clinicians. This set me on fire; I wanted to contribute to this transformation during my career. Completing a residency was the best way to lay a foundation of success, but I needed help in making myself a good candidate. I reached out to one of my professors; to my surprise, he asked to set up a meeting! He told me grades are not everything and encouraged me to get involved, seek mentors, and learn as much as I could from each experience. His guidance was insightful, practical, and motivating. Knowing that someone believed in me was powerful fuel. I became more comfortable asking for help.

Another professor invited me to work on his federally funded research study and helped me publish the paper in a peer-reviewed journal. My Dean and the Director of Pharmacy at Iowa gave me valuable information about administrative residencies and wrote letters of recommendation. These relationships remain strong today, and we continue to stay in touch. Their guidance provided essential experience and made me a competitive candidate for residency programs.

Identify potential mentors, introduce yourself and develop a relationship, ask for help when you need it, and stay in touch. Find people you respect and wish to emulate as well as ones who spur your passion. Asking someone for guidance is the beginning of a mentor relationship that, if cultivated and nurtured, can last a lifetime. Mentors will listen, advise, open up doors, and always have your back. The benefit you gain is reciprocated to the mentor, creating a synergistic relationship. Thank your mentors every chance you get. Let them know how much they mean to you. Simply keeping mentors updated on your progress and sending an occasional note goes a long way. You are a product of their guidance; work hard and make them proud.

Be vulnerable with those you trust, share your struggles, accept failure and learn from it, and continue to grow. I thought I knew what "busy" was until I became a resident. Two years of 80-hour work weeks, classes in the evenings, school projects, research projects, side projects, committees, and … oh, that other thing … a life? At Kansas, I learned what hard work was all about and loved every moment of it. Well, maybe not the moments when I was panicking at 3AM working on a project due later that morning. The first 6 months were rough. Being forced into a group of new peers is uncomfortable. Going from zero to light speed on a steep learning curve is unsettling at best.

Nearing my breaking point, I learned the value of vulnerability. I shared an office with my two administrative co-residents. I had trouble bonding with them because it felt a little like a competition—and that's normal. We were trained to think this way. Only a certain number of people get into pharmacy school, and only a certain number get into a residency. We are lean, mean, competitive machines, which doesn't go away once residency starts. Naturally, we try to be perfect and please everyone around us.

I felt tension between my co-residents, and it was making things worse. One day, I spun my chair around and let loose. I admitted I was having a tough time, lacking sleep, and disappointing myself. I also felt like I was disappointing others. This confession opened the floodgates; they shared their struggles. As simple as it sounds, this was the best medicine. It was comforting to know that they felt the same way, and it gave me confidence to continue. From that point on, we were no longer competing because we were a team.

Be vulnerable and reach out to your peers, your boss, your program director, and others you trust. They will listen and support you. You are going to fail at some point so just accept it. You got into pharmacy school for a reason and are probably used to succeeding at most things. When you fail, you have the power to control how you handle it. If you know yourself, you can begin to understand those feelings. Recognize those emotions, allow them to remain for a short period of time, and then put them behind you. Failure is learning. Learning is growth. This applies to every facet of life. Accept it, learn from it, and forge ahead.

Understand your strengths and weaknesses, talk about them often, and leverage the power of a diverse team. Early in residency, we completed the Strength's Finder test and began our journey toward self-awareness. Some strengths I understood, but others didn't make sense. Slowly, I began to notice these characteristics manifest in myself. They were vastly different compared to my co-residents' strengths, but this was a wonderful realization. I excelled in thinking outside of the box and putting ideas into action. Others were better at analysis and would challenge ideas so they could be refined. Some were best at implementation, so that when ideas were finalized they were exceptionally executed. Understanding the areas we each excelled in, and those we didn't, made us stronger. We worked together and supported each other. This type of synergy is something special.

Take time to truly understand yourself including strengths, weaknesses, tendencies, and beliefs. Personality tests (e.g., Strength's Finder, Myers-Briggs, DISC) and consistent self-reflection are great ways to initiate this process. Talk about them often with your colleagues and encourage them to share theirs too. It may help if you offer up your characteristics first. Self-awareness is the foundation of growth. The more you understand yourself and the people around you, the more satisfied and successful you will be … together.

Identify and cultivate a "super-niche." Developing an area of expertise is extremely important. This may come as a natural progression in your career or happen serendipitously. As a student, I was fortunate to complete a rotation at the ASHP headquarters in Bethesda, Maryland. My preceptor was the Director of Pharmacy Informatics and Technology, and I was assigned a project to assist the newly founded PHIT Collaborative in identifying SNOMED CT (Systematized Nomenclature of Medicine—Clinical Terms) codes for documenting clinical pharmacy services in electronic health records. I did a lot of research on pharmaceutical care, health information technology (IT), health IT standards, interoperability, federally sponsored quality initiatives, clinical quality measure reporting, and other informatics topics, all of which were foreign to me. My passion was ignited again, and I wanted to share what I learned with everyone. I discussed my discoveries with my preceptor and learned more through his guidance and mentorship. My preceptor and I eventually co-authored a paper about what I learned on my rotation. I stayed involved with the project and the PHIT Collaborative after graduating from pharmacy school and into residency. After my residency, I continued to help with the project as a contractor. Recently, I transitioned from a traditional pharmacy administrator job into a project manager consultant role with the Collaborative.

Developing and maintaining a niche should be incorporated into your career plan. Having a specialty area differentiates you as an expert and can lead to speaking opportunities, job offers, and recognition; it ultimately helps to advance your career. However, I would recommend taking it one step further by developing a "super-niche." You may think your niche is pediatrics after completing a PGY2 and passing the Board Certified Pediatric Pharmacy Specialist (BCPPS) exam. A super-niche would be specializing in cystic fibrosis or neonatal parenteral nutrition. Likewise, if your niche is pharmacy administration, you could research and publish on intravenous admixture robotics or using Lean Six Sigma in the medication-use process. Maybe you could blaze a trail in a new area of pharmacy. Fostering your super-niche is exciting, but identifying your super-niche is hard. Investigating areas that you are passionate about and identifying mentors in those areas can be extremely helpful.

Take risks and identify opportunities to grow outside of your comfort zone. My first job after residency was at the Augusta University Medical Center. I wanted to leave the Midwest and experience something totally new. When I moved to Georgia, the only person I knew was the one who hired me. I felt like a fish out of water. It took time to understand the culture and social norms, which influenced building relationships with my employees and colleagues. I had to make friends in the Augusta community through organizations, sports, and other activities. It was a challenging but an incredibly rewarding experience.

Don't be afraid to take a risk. Identify and dive into opportunities that help you grow as a professional and person. These experiences will be specific to your situation. Maybe this means joining a local Toastmasters club to improve your speaking skills, volunteering to serve meals at a homeless shelter, or taking on a new role or responsibility with your current employer. No comfort exists within a growth zone, and no growth occurs within your comfort zone.

Hopefully you will find this advice pertinent and helpful in your current and future experiences. There will always be areas or skills you could improve. I should call my mentors more often, continue to foster my clinical knowledge, read more, improve my speaking skills, and get more sleep. But I'm working on it. You're always working on it. The point is to experience, reflect, learn, and grow constantly. Eventually, you'll be the one doing the mentoring. Enjoy the ride.

Best regards,

Samm

Jennifer (Jen) L. Austin, PharmD

Planning and Opening a New Hospital Pharmacy and Having Broad-Based Impact

Jen shares how the skills she learned in the Pharmacy Leadership Academy have been a game changer, moving her into a director position at a new facility and creating the pharmacy department and services from the ground up. The senior leadership made it clear that everyone would be required to perform in different roles and break down the traditional departmental silos, which were challenges she found both stimulating and fun.

Jennifer (Jen) L. Austin is currently Pharmacy Manager, St. Joseph's Hospital-North, BayCare Health System in Tampa, Florida. Previously she was Pharmacy Operations Manager, St. Joseph's Hospital, and St. Joseph's Children's Hospital in Tampa. She is a faculty member in the Pharmacy Leadership Academy. Jen received her PharmD from Nova Southeastern University and completed a pharmacy practice residency at University of Florida Health Jacksonville.

Jen's advice to young pharmacists who are considering a leadership position is: ***Through development of new leadership skills and organizational awareness, it is possible to help many more patients than you ever could as an individual practitioner.***

Dear Young Pharmacist,

Congratulations on your accomplishments! Through your curiosity, perseverance, and resilience, you are now a part of our wonderful profession. These important traits will lead you to more opportunities than you can imagine. Even though I am still in the midst of my own personal and professional development, I hope to share some thoughts and experiences I've had that may help as you begin your journey.

I will start this conversation by recognizing and thanking my loving, supportive family and the many mentors, sponsors, and dear friends I've had at every stage of my career. These relationships have been vital to my development, and I am paying this forward through supporting others as they move through their careers. I will always be grateful for those who have taken a chance on me at pivotal transition points and the wonderful teams I have been honored to work with and learn from so far. With this, my first suggestion is to *take the time throughout your career to make connections, serve others, and seek out guidance from a broad circle of people you trust*. These relationships and experiences will bring meaning to your days well beyond any accolades you receive for individual accomplishments. In times of challenge, it will also help you keep a fresh perspective and enable you (or have others there to remind you) to see things beyond your immediate circumstances.

Today, I am the Pharmacy Manager in a mid-size community hospital within a large health system. This is not at all what I had originally planned, but it is in line with my passion to improve patient care through pharmacy practice. During pharmacy school, the variety of practice settings and opportunities available to pharmacists continually surprised me. Ultimately, I was drawn toward inpatient clinical practice and decided to pursue a pharmacy practice residency that prepared me well for my first job as a clinical pharmacist. This training also provided exposure to pharmacy operations across the continuum of care, administrative projects, and committee experiences. They became the foundation for my eventual shift in interest to patient care contributions on a broader scale through leadership roles. When a position opened up on our leadership team a few years later, I knew I did not have the formal training or experience to apply but asked for additional projects during the interim period. This soon led to an Operations Coordinator position and eventually a role as Manager. Initially, I was torn over possibly losing the clinical knowledge I had worked so hard to learn, but I realized that I would not lose my understanding of what pharmacists are capable of bringing to patient care and the value of a strong clinical practice. Through development of new leadership skills and organizational awareness, I could help others help many more patients than I ever could as an individual practitioner.

Locally and through professional organizations, I had many great leaders to learn from during these transitions. I took advantage of numerous leadership-based continuing education programs and also benefitted from my employer's leadership training programs. Although they were all helpful, I wanted more formalized pharmacy-focused leadership training; however, pausing my career for a practice management residency or going back to school were not reasonable options for me.

Near that time, I learned about a new program being offered by the ASHP Research and Education Foundation called the Pharmacy Leadership Academy. This comprehensive, online group of courses was led by recognized pharmacy leaders and covered a wide range of topics—the perfect supplement to my on-the-job training experience. This year-long leadership program offered course presentations, readings, journaling exercises, and case assignments that were immediately applicable to my responsibilities. The faculty was engaging, challenging, and inspiring. They helped me gain a deeper understanding of how to effectively align pharmacy practice initiatives with organizational goals and how to employ a variety of change management principles for safety and quality advancement. Not only was it invaluable to interact with other participants who were facing similar practice challenges, but through our live discussion calls and threaded discussions they opened my eyes to a wider variety of practice settings and different approaches to providing high-quality patient care.

Simultaneous to my Academy experience, I worked on a team to plan for a new facility within our organization. This was a wonderful opportunity to apply lessons learned and innovation to the physical design of the pharmacy and practice model and to enhance safety and efficiency through the introduction of greater automation support than was previously utilized in our pharmacies. The sessions for planning our departmental and interdisciplinary workflows and design of our new electronic health record provided venues for garnering support for our clinical practice while gaining an even greater understanding of how we could best champion multidisciplinary patient care and organizational success.

In the earliest stages of the project, I knew we were building a state-of-the-art facility, but I wasn't planning to apply for the transfer partly because I had a bias toward the smaller bed size compared to where I had previously trained and worked. I was torn once again over the thought of deviating from my current practice and what I thought was the acceptable path for career development. The more I interacted with the other Academy participants in leadership roles in like-sized facilities, however, I began to appreciate that fewer people and patients did not equate to lesser responsibility. To the contrary, it became clear that I would be stretched to expand my skills to include all elements of pharmacy leadership responsibilities and the need to engage everyone on the pharmacy team to their fullest capacity. It also meant that I would be stretched beyond pharmacy practice because every leader in the facility would need to be engaged in virtually every organizational effort. Our senior leadership emphasized that everyone had to assume multiple roles and break down traditional departmental silos to provide the top-decile quality of care and performance we expected. Our patients deserved nothing less, and our health system deserved a highly reliable contributor given the investment that was being made. I was hooked, shell-shocked on occasion by the magnitude and number of tasks at hand, but hooked nonetheless.

After the planning came to an end and it was time to make things happen, we drew on every didactic experience, practical lesson learned, and support we could on a moment-to-moment basis. We were overwhelmed by the sheer number of team members to be recruited and on boarded, new technical systems to be implemented and learned, workflows to be established simultaneously across all departments on top of culture building, frequent regulatory oversight, organizational scrutiny, and above all the responsibility to care for our patients. But it was always incredibly rewarding. I would have missed this career highlight and many others with this special team of practitioners and leaders had I not been exposed to other ways of thinking and willingness to step out of my comfort zone. This leads to my second suggestion: *keep investing in your learning even if you have been in your role for a long time.* My third suggestion is to *take a chance on a new experience or change in direction, knowing that you can always make another change if it doesn't work out.* In each instance, you will undoubtedly grow from the experience no matter what the outcome.

In the years after the opening, we continued to meet the challenges of expedient growth of our facility and health system in a rapidly changing healthcare environment. This certainly has provided new layers of challenge and opportunity as we work, like many of you, to standardize processes across facilities at all levels and grow into the accountable care organization and population health management arenas. Today is also an exciting time for pharmacy practice as we pursue provider status and begin to see new roles for pharmacists across the healthcare continuum. Now more than ever we need leaders at all levels in our practice settings and our professional organizations to advance and improve patient care through pharmacy practice. There is no shortage of venues to gain leadership training and opportunities no matter where you are in your career.

Through sharing some of my experiences, I hope you find comfort in whatever path you follow to your leadership role.

I wish you much joy in your journey!

Jen

Udobi C. Campbell, PharmD, MBA

Don't Turn Down Opportunities Even If They Make You Feel Uncomfortable

Udobi, who froze the first time she had to speak in front of people, shares this story to show how she used it in improving her communication skills. She believes if you let these opportunities for growth and development pass you by because you are uncomfortable, you will never fully realize her potential. Udobi also explains how she and her husband are both career driven and integrate their lives with those of their two daughters.

Udobi C. Campbell is currently Associate Chief Pharmacy Officer and previously was Assistant Director of Pharmacy at Duke University Hospital. She has served on the ASHP Section of Pharmacy Practice Managers' Advisory Group on Leadership Development and the University Health System Consortium Medication-Use Informatics and Technology Committee. Udobi received her MBA from the Duke University Fuqua School of Business and her PharmD from Florida A&M University. She completed a pharmacy practice residency at Duke University Medical Center.

Udobi offers the following advice for young pharmacists: **Take opportunities even if they make you uncomfortable; it is possible to have a progressive career and also be engaged on the home front by relying on support from family and friends.**

Dear Young Pharmacist,

Are you wondering how to get from point A of your career to point B? Do you find yourself admiring others and wishing you were on the same career path? Do you get energized at times or grow weary about your own potential? If this sounds like you, just remember you are not alone. The possibilities for professional growth, regardless of how you define it, are conceivable from whatever point you are at today. The profession of pharmacy and the expectations of those who practice it are growing at a fast pace; it is incumbent on all of us to expand our knowledge, abilities, and horizon for the betterment of not just ourselves but also our affiliated professional organizations and patients.

The pursuit for administrative leadership in pharmacy became my goal about 10 years ago. Although I have not yet attained my ideal position, I am content with the level achieved so far. In the following passages, I will reveal some key things that have been remarkably impactful in my career.

"If we're growing, we're always going to be out of our comfort zone." Those simple, yet profound words by John Maxwell seem to define most of my life. Did I know or even fully understand that quote in my younger days? No. But in later years, as I habitually self-reflected, I came to accept that personal and professional growth requires operating outside our comfort zone. In fact, it's how I try to live every day. Allow me to share a hallmark experience from my earlier years that has been influential in my growth as a person, wife, mother, and pharmacy leader.

The ability to communicate via written word, verbal expression, or body language is a critical skill for pharmacy leaders. As I lament to my students and mentees, how we choose to communicate speaks volumes about who we are as people, how confident we are, what insecurities we harbor, and how we measure on the trust scale. My interest and passion for communication has grown over the years. I have immense admiration for those who consistently do it well, and I enjoy speaking to groups. It is partly because of this passion that I was motivated to pursue academia as an Assistant Professor at Hampton University School of Pharmacy following my postgraduate year (PGY) 1 residency in 2001. It is this passion that compelled me to volunteer when leaders at my institution, Duke University Hospital, were asked to help teach all employees about a new model of communication to be used, particularly with patients, their loved ones, and each other. And this passion also drives me to accept invitations quickly for speaking engagements.

So how did this intense attraction to the art of communication and speaking develop? It did not develop the way you might think. It was 1992, and I was a very timid 11th grader enrolled in an English 101 course at Florida A&M University in Tallahassee. I was the only high school student in the class. As if that wasn't strange enough, I wore my high school uniform when I attended classes. Everything about the class was great; at some point during the semester, each student had to make an oral presentation. I remember my turn as if it were yesterday. I exited my desk while slowly rubbing my right palm across it. Proceeding cautiously, I walked to the front of the room, turning to face the students only to find countless eyeballs focused intensely on me. I could not utter a single word! I just stared. Yes, I froze much like a statue. As innocent as I was, that experience has remained one of the lowest and most embarrassing moments of my life.

The famous songwriter Irving Berlin is quoted as saying "Life is 10% what you make it and 90% how you take it." I certainly took this humbling experience as an opportunity to improve. I sought out offers to communicate with a crowd, although uncomfortable, to provide more practice time in front of people. My next big test was delivering the graduation speech as the school valedictorian in 1993. Suffice it to say that my family—most of whom had traveled across the continent to share this milestone moment with me—was incredibly proud. Even today, with every opportunity I get to speak in front of others, no matter the size, I remember my English 101 course experience.

Now ask yourself: How many times have you turned down an opportunity because you didn't feel capable or comfortable, too young for the profession, or too busy? How many times have you not reacted positively to critical feedback on a 360-evaluation but rather took it personally and stalled in your career? These chances for growth and development that you pass by will be quickly picked up by others who understand growth often requires engaging in something uncomfortable. I urge you to actively seek out activities, particularly those that are uncomfortable, to provide the skills you need to perform at that next level.

At the beginning of this letter, I posed the question about whether you admired the career paths of other colleagues. Truth be told, I sometimes wish that I had mentors in the earlier stages of my career. I didn't; as such, I often wonder if my career route would have been different. Numerous articles have been written about the value of mentorship and its benefit for the mentee and the mentor. The best case scenario as it relates to mentorship is to have someone more experienced than you, who recognizes your leadership potential, unselfishly offer to nurture and grow your potential. That, however, is not what happens in reality, so the alternative is for us to approach individuals for guidance and ask them to become sounding boards for the critical decisions we make. In the last few years, I have cultivated relationships with knowledgeable leaders who have helped direct my career path, and I am grateful to them. But equally, I have received counsel from nonprofessionals whose words of encouragement have filled the gap when necessary. I believe that we should seek variety when it comes to mentors. Men, women, professionals, and nonprofessionals all bring a different perspective to bear, and there is often a completeness that becomes apparent when we consider viewpoints from different angles.

As I ponder how I got to where I am today, particularly professionally, I would be remiss if I didn't mention the incredible support from my husband Samuel Quincy Campbell. In her book, *Lean In*, Sheryl Sandberg, Chief Operating Officer of Facebook, Inc., touched on the impact a spouse has on one's career advancement. In fact, she has been quoted as saying that "The most important career choice you make is who you marry." While the statement might be a bit extreme to some, it certainly carries lots of truths. Luckily, in my case, both my husband and I are very career driven, and we understand and support each other when one of us has to miss a family event due to work-related commitments.

This brings me to the topic of work-life balance or, as I prefer to call it, *work-life integration.* In our 13-year marriage, we have been blessed with two wonderful daughters, Olivia, 7, and Abigail, 5. They are curious girls who request explanations when we fail to participate in an event; but, thus far, they have been very understanding. My hope is that as they grow older, they will recognize, appreciate, and be instilled with the same passion to be excellent at whatever they do. As my responsibilities as a leader have expanded over the years, I have struggled with accepting "balance" as what we do in these situations. I believe that it is, and ought to be, a give-and-take relationship. There has to be a willingness to sacrifice on both sides. Is it possible to have a progressive career and also be well engaged on the home front? Absolutely, but it often requires that we employ support from our family and friends.

I ask you again, are you wondering how to get from point A of your career to point B? I trust that I have added to the tools in your career toolbox as you seek to answer this question. Remember that growth may at times be unsettling, and that it is okay; enrich yourself through relationships with mentors and accept the support from friends and family. Our profession, our organizations, and our patients are depending on us to do our part.

Sincerely,

Udobi

Delia Charest Carias, PharmD, BCPS

Sometimes Others Know You Better Than You Know Yourself

Many of us can describe with great precision how we came to choose pharmacy as our life's work. Yet for some of our colleagues, it is almost as if the profession of pharmacy *chose them*. Such is the case with Delia, a rising star from Mississippi and the daughter of two pharmacists. Despite having the utmost respect for her pharmacist parents and their chosen profession, Delia had no intention of following in their footsteps when she began her college career as a music major. While pursuing her degree, she worked as a part-time pharmacy technician, which exposed her to the profession and ignited her interest in pharmacy. The rest, as they say, is history . . . in the making.

Delia Charest Carias is currently Medication Use Policy Coordinator at St. Jude Children's Research Hospital. Delia received her PharmD degree from Samford University, McWhorter School of Pharmacy. She completed a postgraduate year (PGY) 1 residency at Johns Hopkins Hospital and a PGY2 specialty residency in pharmacy administration at Methodist University Hospital in Memphis, Tennessee. She is an active member and involved volunteer in ASHP, the Pediatric Infectious Diseases Society, and the American College of Clinical Pharmacy.

Delia's advice is: ***Sometimes it is necessary to look through the eyes of others to learn our true path.***

Dear Young Pharmacist,

Growing up as the child of two pharmacists, I knew at a young age exactly what I wanted to do with my life—be a musician. Despite my parent's constant coaxing to look at pharmacy as a career, I knew what I wanted to do and no one could tell me otherwise. The first step involved moving out of state to pursue training.

Moving out of state did not come at a cheap price; living on my own meant I needed a job. As a full-time music major, I needed something with flexible hours that could fit around my schedule. Again, my parents suggested I look into pharmacy. Although I had successfully avoided working in my father's community drug store while I was growing up, I thought working in pharmacy now might be a good idea.

I was lucky enough to find a job as a pharmacy technician at a local pharmacy near my apartment. It wasn't long before I wanted to know all about the medications. I would call my mother nightly when I got off work and ask about specific medications, what they were used for, and how they worked in the body. For the first time, I was interested in the stories she would tell about her days at the hospital. In addition, I was reading pharmacy journals in my spare time. This is when I knew I had "a problem." I came to the realization that maybe this pharmacy thing was for me; maybe my parents had been right all along. Because I was over half-way finished with my music degree, I decided to complete it while getting my prerequisites for pharmacy school. I took summer and night classes and finished in 4 years. My parents were ecstatic to have me follow in what we call our family business, and I can now admit that they were right all along.

Growing up, I was lucky to see both the community and hospital settings of the profession. This exposure allowed me to enter pharmacy school knowing exactly the career I wanted. My parents were well respected in their chosen fields, my father with his community pharmacy practice and my mother serving as a clinical pharmacist in a hospital long before it became a common practice. While I admired my father, it was my mother's career—being part of the medical team and interacting with patients to improve their care—that fascinated me.

My passion was further strengthened while working at the University of Alabama at Birmingham Hospital (UAB) as a pre-pharmacy and pharmacy student. UAB had a wonderful summer program, which allowed students to work as pharmacy technicians full time and shadow a clinical pharmacist 1–2 days a week. I spent time shadowing pharmacists in oncology, transplant, and various critical care units. During this time, I fell in love with the medical critical care unit.

So, it was settled; during my first year of pharmacy school, I had a goal to become a critical care clinical pharmacist. I knew it was going to be difficult, and that I needed to do well in pharmacy school and complete 2 years of postgraduate residency. I was up for the challenge. I loaded up my fourth year rotations with as many critical care rotations as allowed. However, despite knowing my path, I decided that fourth year rotations would be a perfect time to take advantage of my uncle's proximity to Washington, DC. In addition to my required and critical care elective rotations, I asked for rotations in our nation's capital and was excited to get three: with the Food and Drug Administration (FDA), National Cancer Institute (NCI), and ASHP. The first of these rotations was at ASHP.

Honestly, I did not expect to enjoy the rotation at ASHP as much as I did. Everyone at headquarters was warm and welcoming, not at all what a girl from the Deep South expected of her first time in such a big city. ASHP showed me a side of pharmacy that I never knew existed—where pharmacists help other pharmacists to improve patient care by creating programs and advocating for our profession. There was so much more to ASHP than I realized as a pharmacy student; from advocacy to professional policies and practice standards to residency training, ASHP was involved in every aspect of hospital pharmacy. I spent that month learning from thought leaders in our profession and working countless hours on projects for various sections within the organization. I found satisfaction in creating resources, which would be used on a daily basis to improve patient care. I enjoyed my time there so much that I volunteered to continue working with the ASHP staff on a special project even after my rotation ended. I had a new appreciation for my association and their support of pharmacists.

My appreciation for organizational management continued to grow as I spent time at the FDA and NCI. I saw how pharmacists engaged in federal policy development and clinical trial design. I worked on meaningful projects while continuing my education and working alongside committed pharmacists. But the rotations eventually ended, and I continued on my journey to become a critical care clinical pharmacist. I knew that what I learned from these experiences improved me as a pharmacist and ultimately would benefit my future patients.

When residency match day arrived, I couldn't believe I matched at Johns Hopkins Hospital in Baltimore, Maryland! I could not think of a better place to continue my education. Like any residency, the learning curve was steep. I remember spending many late nights at the office reviewing patients and disease states. I knew when I finished, all of the hard work would be worth it. The day soon came when early commitments for PGY2 programs were due. I submitted my application to stay at Hopkins as a PGY2 specialty resident. My application was declined, and my world came crashing down. Little did I realize, my preceptors knew me better than I knew myself. As I thought about what to do in the coming year, I sought counsel from a few close pharmacy preceptors. Through these discussions, I realized I had known my path for a long time. The rotations I enjoyed the most were not on the floors and units but the ones where I developed programs, completed projects, and worked with people outside of the pharmacy. In fact, I discovered that during my PGY1 residency interview, one of my future preceptors questioned my intention for a PGY2 in critical care when "I so clearly should have been doing administration."

I went on to complete a PGY2 health-system pharmacy administration residency at Methodist University Hospital in Memphis, Tennessee. I found the joy and excitement that I remembered experiencing in my fourth year rotations. I found my calling! On finishing my second year residency, I was fortunate enough to be hired at St. Jude Children's Research Hospital. My position as the Coordinator of Medication Use Policy is the perfect mix of my interests and skills. What I do impacts the lives of each of our kids—maybe not directly on rounds—but indirectly through the programs, projects, and system improvements I work to implement every day. Using the skills I have developed to improve patient care brings me joy.

I have learned many lessons during my short pharmacy career, but one of the most important is that sometimes others know you better than you know yourself. As pharmacists, we are trained to be confident in our decisions. Our profession has trained us that if we work hard and strive for excellence, we will achieve our dreams. I still believe it is true. However, sometimes we should look through the eyes of others to learn our true calling.

Regards,

Delia

Rick Couldry, RPh, MS, FASHP

Although Not Easy, a Guy Can Have It All—Family and Successful Career

Rick explains that in addition to the typical things a pharmacist leader has in his office, a few others such as photos of his family probably go unnoticed but are more important to him. Rick outlines how he is integrating his family life with his career. He also discusses how he is engaging staff and leaders at *eight* locations versus one while not letting the rest of his work suffer.

Rick Couldry is currently Executive Director, Pharmacy Services, and Residency Director of the combined MS-health system pharmacy administration postgraduate year (PGY) 2 program at The University of Kansas Hospital. Previously, he was Director of Pharmacy. He is Chair, ASHP Section of Pharmacy Practice Managers. Rick received his BS in Pharmacy from the University of Missouri–Kansas City and his MS in Hospital Pharmacy Administration from The University of Kansas. He completed a 2-year administrative residency at The University of Kansas Hospital.

Rick's advice is: **Don't sacrifice time with your family because you can't get it back. Decide where you will make sacrifices when you can't do it all or say "yes" to everything. Find and sustain your perspective on what is truly important to you and let that be your guide.**

Dear Young Pharmacist,

When you walk into my office, you will see many things you would see in any office such as diplomas, art, and licenses. Of all the items, a few that probably go unnoticed are the most important to me—a mouse pad with a picture of me and my young daughter walking hand-in-hand, a photo of my 5-year old son wearing a t-shirt and tie in a cheesy frame that he labeled Happy Father's Day, and a photograph of my beaming bride in her wedding gown. I really enjoy having these items there where all kinds of meetings, decisions, mentoring, and work happen. Although many aspects of success are important, these treasured mementos are constant reminders that not all of them are directly related to leadership, pharmacy, or healthcare.

I have been fortunate that my mentors have given me great advice. Often, it was related to not letting your family life slip in deference to work success. I remember, quite vividly, one of these discussions. It was at a hotel in Orlando at a Midyear Clinical Meeting. In a fortunate moment of solitude, between the conference's many demands, I found myself at the hotel bar with a successful, widely recognized pharmacy leader. As we sat and talked, she asked what was on my mind. I told her I wondered if I was doing all I should to serve pharmacy and to uphold and advance the legacy of pharmacy leadership. I told her that my peers were advancing by giving more talks, being elected to national positions, and writing more articles than me. I didn't feel like I was doing enough. I went on to tell her how I was torn between doing more and being a good dad. My daughter was 4 at the time, and my wife and I were expecting our second child. She asked me a lot about my family and what I was doing at work and for the profession. One of her questions was so simple and powerful, I have never forgotten it: "Do you think in a few years when your kids are more grown up that pharmacy *won't* have a need for leaders?" I was speechless. I stammered, finally, "I guess I never thought of it that way." She just smiled, nodded, and said "Don't sacrifice time with your family. You can't get it back. There's never a shortage of opportunities for good leaders."

I have lived by those words ever since, but making them work has not been easy. I sometimes find myself focusing on who got elected to a position, who is chairing a committee, and all those pictures on social media of people touring international pharmacy sites and attending conferences. These things push and nag at you. Even harder is receiving a request from a colleague who wants me to attend a conference or give a talk. It gets harder when the colleague is someone close to me—a friend, someone you never want to let down. So, of course, sometimes (actually, many times) the answer is "yes." I keep mental track of my "yes" responses. A funny thing about them is that I often feel like I haven't done a lot, but when I review my list of accomplishments it's fairly significant. Occasionally, I need outsiders to give me perspective. One such person was a Senior Director at ASHP with whom I often worked. When I confided my concerns about my contributions, he laughed—not judging me but in empathy. He had struggled with the same feelings. We have continued to share stories and parenting tips, and he's often told me he appreciates our talks because they happen so infrequently.

Another area where professional and family responsibilities often collide is with meetings. For example, my daughter's birthday is in early June, so it always conflicts with pharmacy meetings. I've had to fly in for one day, fulfill my obligations, and fly back out to make things work. Friends, past residents, alumni, and others I want to catch up with are all surprised at my early departure. Over the years, they have gotten used to it, but I feel torn by wanting to stay and spend time with old friends, do more work, and have fun. But I know my daughter Grace would never understand why I missed her birthday, and there are precious few when she absolutely wants me to be there. So I always find myself smiling on that early flight home. The "quick conference" also works when business trips have been too frequent; I feel the need just to be home, even if a critical event is not pulling me back. Finding time for soccer and basketball games, school awards, and date nights with my wife is also essential.

It's important for leaders to think of having a whole-life perspective. An ideal way to do this is to lead by example. The reaction I get from others when I am doing the "quick conference," taking a call on the drive home or rearranging a meeting to go to an event at the school, is respect. It also empowers those you are leading to do the same without fear of judgment or retribution. This perspective is honestly appreciated and tends to increase loyalty and commitment from others. It makes your team stronger and more successful.

Career success can make doing this even harder. I have been blessed with the opportunity to serve in positions with ever-increasing responsibility and scope. At the same time, my organization has experienced double-digit growth almost every year for a decade. This has made my work exciting, engaging, and rewarding. However, it has also put additional pressures on my efforts to maintain that work-life balance. I have had to find time to learn entirely new aspects of pharmacy practice and new models of the pharmacy business. After you learn them, you have the real work ahead of you by figuring out how to get them approved, implemented, and operating on an ongoing basis.

In my current role as Pharmacy Executive, new expectations have emerged as a member of the executive team: hosting events, rounding with staff during weekends and evenings, being an on-call administrator for the health system, and investing the time to develop new relationships.

Because I have a larger and more diverse group of people, it is a constant challenge to find quality time to spend with them. A further complicating factor has been that instead of having one location, I now have eight. So how can you engage staff and leaders at eight locations and honestly give them the time and commitment that they deserve, while not letting the rest of your work suffer? I'm still figuring it out. There are no silver bullets.

An important lesson is to know when you stop owning something. Supporting the development of your team by helping prepare them to *own* responsibilities and then giving them that ownership is essential. This helps the team grow and develop, offers them new and challenging opportunities, and allows you to manage your own time and responsibilities.

Don't forget your home team, too. My wife and kids deserve the same kind of communication and participation in what is happening with our family. We have lots of family discussions about my job, responsibilities, travel, and other expectations. Just like the work team, I have had to stop owning things. For example, outsourcing lawn care and some pet care were expenses we added to our family budget so we could better manage tasks and have the family time that we wanted.

Striking a balance between career and family is not easy. You have to decide what you want from different aspects of your life and have a clear idea of how you will define your success. Determine where to make sacrifices when you can't do it all or say "yes" to everything. Find and sustain your perspective on what is truly important to you and let that be your guide. Most important, you must not think it's easy or that you don't have to work at it. *You do*. Go your own way and be happy with your decision. It is one of the many tough things that leaders do.

All the best,

Rick

Kristine R. Crews, PharmD, BCPS, FCCP

Your Contribution May Be in a Field That Has Not Yet Been Imagined

Kristine traces her clinical scientist career development, including how she and her husband manage two busy careers and raise three children. She describes the pharmacist-run, multi-disciplinary personalized medicine service at St. Jude Children's Research Hospital that conducts upfront pharmacogenetics testing on all patients.

Kristine R. Crews is currently Translational Research Laboratory Director, Pharmaceutical Department, St. Jude Children's Research Hospital, and Program Director, ASHP-accredited postgraduate year (PGY) 2 residency in clinical pharmacogenetics. She is Assistant Professor, Department of Pharmacy, College of Pharmacy, University of Tennessee Health Science Center. Kristine received her BS in Pharmacy and PharmD degree from Rutgers University. She completed a pharmacy practice residency and a clinical pharmacokinetics specialty residency at the University of Kentucky Chandler Medical Center. Following her residencies, she completed a 2-year fellowship in clinical pharmacokinetics and pharmacodynamics at the University of North Carolina and Glaxo Wellcome, Inc.

Kristine's advice is: **Be open to what the future brings and don't be bound by the choices for your career path that you can see currently. Your most exciting contribution may ultimately be in a field that has not yet been imagined.**

Dear Young Pharmacist,

We practice pharmacy at an exciting time. Advances in targeted agents and new, more specific diagnostic tools allow us to personalize a patient's therapy with improved outcomes. What will pharmacy practice look like in the next 20 years? We can't even imagine the breakthroughs and innovations to come. The one thing we know is that the roles of pharmacists will change with the changing landscape. I practice in the relatively new field of clinical pharmacogenetics. On a day-to-day basis, I work with both laboratory-based researchers and clinicians to apply pharmacogenetic research findings to optimize patient care.

Pharmacists have known for a long time that medications do not work the same for everyone. Although most patients may benefit from a particular medication, others may see no effect and still others may suffer harm from a treatment that was intended to improve their health. Pharmacogenetics is the field that seeks to find differences in our genome, which influence how patients respond to specific medications.

Pharmacogenetics research is not very new. Laboratories have been reporting links between genes and treatment-induced toxicity for decades. What *is* new is the area of personalized medicine, which is taking these research findings and applying them as a way to individualize care for a particular patient. Personalized medicine is a broad area; clinical pharmacogenetics is one of the first subspecialties of this discipline to make differences in how patients are treated. At St. Jude Children's Research Hospital, we have implemented an ambitious and comprehensive program that offers upfront pharmacogenetic testing to all patients at our institution early in their therapy and places these preemptive test results into the patients' electronic health record to optimize the use of certain medications if they are needed. When one of these drugs is ordered, clinical decision support alerts let the prescriber know if the patient's genotype might impact his or her ability to respond to treatment. Pharmacists run this multidisciplinary, personalized medicine service and educate other clinicians in interpreting genotype results to individualize therapy.

Clinical pharmacogenetics, however, was not a specialty one could choose when I was a pharmacy student. Instead, I got involved in pharmacokinetics research as a PharmD student in the laboratory of Dr. Patty Fan-Havard at Rutgers University; it was an experience that sparked my love of research. Dr. Fan-Havard was the first of many strong mentors throughout my training who instilled in me both clinical pharmacy skills and the drive to ask and answer research questions. As a resident at the University of Kentucky, I worked with Dr. Mary H.H. Ensom, a clinical pharmacokineticist, who was a model for excellence in teaching, mentoring, and running a clinical pharmacokinetics service. During my residency, I heard Dr. Bill Evans from St. Jude speak about his innovative pharmacogenetics research of mercaptopurine in children with acute lymphoblastic leukemia. He told of how he and his collaborators had discovered that patients with one or two copies of a nonfunctional *TPMT* gene were at high risk of toxicity to mercaptopurine and shared data showing that upfront knowledge of the patient's genotype allowed the mercaptopurine dose to be decreased to safe and effective levels. I was inspired by his groundbreaking research. I suddenly knew that I wanted to work in an environment where translational research would be valued.

At the end of our 2 years of residency, my classmates pursued clinical or clinical faculty positions, but I knew this was not my calling. Eager to continue learning how to integrate research into a clinical pharmacy career, I pursued a fellowship with Dr. Kim Brouwer at the University of North Carolina. I learned about drug development and clinical pharmacokinetics trials, spending a year in the clinical pharmacology group at Glaxo Wellcome, Inc. The training paid off in a big way. As I was finishing my fellowship training, I spotted a job listing for St. Jude Children's Research Hospital. Dr. Evans was hiring a clinical pharmacist with clinical trials training and knowledge of pharmacokinetics and drug development. Implausibly, I was hired right out of my fellowship and have spent my career practicing translational research at St. Jude.

The culture of St. Jude Children's Research Hospital is one that values innovation and collaboration. The mission of the pharmaceutical department, under the leadership of Dr. Mary Relling, is to deliver the highest quality comprehensive clinical pharmaceutical care to children with catastrophic diseases, always working to integrate research findings into clinical care as quickly as possible. I found a way to play a small role in this greater mission.

As a pharmacy student looking toward my future, I had two major goals for my life. One was to be a clinical scientist, work in a laboratory, and make discoveries that would improve care for patients. Beyond that, I wanted to have a houseful of kids of my own. I'm from a big Polish-Catholic family; for me, a happy life means being surrounded by many loved ones. Now, more than 20 years out of pharmacy school, my husband and I have demanding careers and a noisy house filled with three busy, talented kids. It has taken a lot to build our dream. As all working parents know, it is a continual challenge to integrate family life and career. Navigating both successfully has required striking a balance that works for me, keeping my values at the core of what I do at home and at work. As a mother, I don't have the luxury of putting in late evenings at the office (even though these are the hours that I am most productive). My evening hours are devoted to kids and their activities, to dinner as a family, and to time together. For me, that means I work harder for the hours I *am* at work. Most evenings I work at home for another hour or two after soccer practices, piano lessons, dinner, homework, and bedtimes are over. When I go to conferences, I plan my schedule carefully to limit my travel to two nights away from home whenever possible. Any more than that has me missing my family and my family missing matched socks and packed lunches.

Balancing a career and a healthy family life requires living in two worlds and so does working as a translational researcher. To be a translational researcher, you must be comfortable with not fully fitting into either a basic science world or a purely clinical practice but rather acting as a bridge between the two settings. The parts about my job that I love are designing clinical protocols with other collaborators, writing and publishing papers, presenting our work to other clinicians and researchers, and, of course, making a difference in the outcomes of patients.

As a resident and fellow, I trained in clinical pharmacokinetics as a specialty. However, the closely related field of clinical pharmacogenetics has grown in recent years and is now a specialty in its own right. It is no coincidence that this new field is coming of age now. The successful completion of the Human Genome Project a decade ago has accelerated the rate of pharmacogenetic discovery. We know more about the relationships between genes and drugs. In addition, the adoption of electronic health records allows for clinical decision support for pharmacogenetic test results, which is an essential element needed to individualize therapy based on a patient's genetic test results. The combination of high-quality research findings and available technology gives us the ability to tailor a patient's therapy based on clinical pharmacogenetic testing.

Several years ago, our group at St. Jude—under the guidance of Dr. Relling—set out to develop our leading-edge trial to incorporate preemptive pharmacogenetics as standard of care. We had a vision of being leaders in this young field of implementing clinical pharmacogenetics. When we considered who would follow our lead, it was apparent that pharmacists were well positioned to direct such endeavors at other institutions, yet there were few pharmacists at the time with the necessary specialized training. That's when we developed the first PGY2 specialty residency in clinical pharmacogenetics. Our residency, now in its sixth year, trains the next generation of pharmacists to have the skills to implement personalized medicine in other healthcare settings. Our former residents have established themselves as experts in their own right and are forging paths in settings that are as unique as the institutions where they now practice. For those considering a clinical pharmacogenetics position, the skills that are needed are ones many pharmacists already have: a working knowledge of drug metabolism pathways, pharmacokinetic principles, and literature evaluation; the desire to educate patients and clinicians; and the ability to collaborate with a broad range of people. This specialty is one within the reach of many clinical pharmacists.

When I look at my own children, I see unlimited potential. Likewise, when I reflect on the field of clinical pharmacogenetics, I see unlimited horizons. Our growing knowledge and understanding of genomic data will be translated into actionable guidelines for the use of many classes of drugs that will lead to widespread use of preemptive genotyping. Although still in its infancy, it is likely that during your career, clinical pharmacogenetics will allow us to individualize therapy for a wide range of diseases. My message to you is to be open to what the future brings and don't be bound by the choices for your career path that you can see currently. The most exciting contribution you make may ultimately be in a field that has not yet been imagined.

Sincerely,

Kristine

Joseph A. Dikun, PharmD, PhD candidate

Find Your Own Way Even If It Is a Change from Your Original Path

While pursuing his PharmD degree in the inaugural class of a new college of pharmacy, Joe Dikun was so inspired that his white coat felt like a red cape. He crafted a well-reasoned professional plan that included goals, milestones, and a detailed roadmap. Yet, as he approached graduation, he knew something was missing. Joe's professional soul-searching led him to pursue a new direction, which included a PhD program and the ultimate goal of educating others.

Joseph A. Dikun is currently a PhD candidate in Pharmaceutical Sciences at the University of Mississippi School of Pharmacy. He is also a practicing community pharmacist. Joe received his PharmD degree at the Northeast Ohio Medical University and his BS in Biological Sciences at Youngstown State University. He is an active member and volunteer in ASHP, the American Pharmacists Association, the American College of Clinical Pharmacy, and the American Association of Colleges of Pharmacy. He is also a member of Phi Lambda Sigma and the Rho Chi Society.

Joe's advice is: **If what you are doing is not working for you or if your priorities have changed, it's fine to make modifications.**

Dear Young Pharmacist,

Although you may wander, you are far from lost. I often think about my own white coat ceremony—the symbolic transition we all make into our chosen profession—with pride, reflection, and surprise even to this day. Not only was I a member of the inaugural pharmacy class at the Northeast Ohio Medical University, but I had finally found the ideal profession for me. That white coat felt like a red cape, and I was ready to take on the world! I had a plan full of professional goals, drawing a detailed and thoughtful roadmap to success. Along this map, I highlighted the professional stops I would take at 1, 2, 5, 10, and even 20 years from that day. This version of my former self would be surprised to know how little I have figured out even to this day, 5 years into my rewarding career as a pharmacist and currently a full-time PhD student.

As the son of generations of blue-collar workers, some career decisions always seemed quite clear. I knew I would be attending college, fulfilling my mother's dream for her only son. I knew I was expected to capitalize on my God-given talents in the sciences, if not for myself then for others less fortunate. I also knew that my focus should be in finding a career that would provide me with prosperity and stability. But early in my undergraduate experiences, I changed my major from chemical engineering, to pre-medicine, to the biological sciences, and so on. It was always disheartening to watch my contemporaries find their way in occupations they truly loved, while I was still trying to figure it all out.

Luckily, pharmacy found me at exactly the right time. First, a member of the local community and personal acquaintance who recognized my professional angst allowed me to shadow several health-system pharmacists in inpatient and other clinical settings. This opened my eyes to a world I had never been exposed to outside of the more visible roles for pharmacists. Second, I noticed flyers, announcements, and rumblings of a new pharmacy program focused on the inter-professional education of student physicians and pharmacists in the halls of my now alma mater, the Youngstown State University. The faculty's excitement was palpable; the mission and vision of the program aligned with my values and was something with which I could immediately connect. As someone who always yearned to love my chosen profession, these people truly had what it takes to help me in my career choice.

This is where it becomes important to revisit the roadmap I mentioned previously, as I was truly the "man with a plan." Throughout my pharmacy education, individuals in my personal and professional lives had heard my elevator speech many times and knew I was pursuing training in a postgraduate year (PGY) 1/PGY2/Master of Science degree in health-system pharmacy administration residency program. In addition, my service to the profession on a local, state, and national level were all preparing me for these kinds of opportunities. Despite my experiences up to this point, something was missing as I headed into my last professional year. Providing clinical services or more traditional dispensing services were not fulfilling anymore. Several questions plagued me:

- Why was an individual patient encounter increasingly less satisfying than global discussions of public policy and healthcare utilization?

- Why, when my colleagues were excited from learning all they could about the latest medication to hit the market, was I more concerned about potential coverage, formulary decisions, and access issues?

- Why were unanswered questions about the behaviors of patients, pharmacists, and student pharmacists keeping me up at night?

- Why was I thinking about the best way to educate the next generation of pharmacists when I should be considering how to best educate my patients on making optimal use of their medications?

It was hard *not* to feel like I was making a terrible mistake in my career path, or possibly I was just burned out. Nonetheless, I had some thinking to do. Hours of honest reflection, consultation with mentors, and difficult conversations led me to one conclusion—it was time to start over and pursue my PhD in pharmacy administration. I felt like it was the right choice for me (and probably for many others who may not be willing to admit it). If your priorities have changed, it's ok to make modifications. I challenge students and young pharmacists to ask themselves questions throughout their experience:

- Are you more interested in a career producing knowledge or consuming knowledge?

- Do you see the world in a more macro- or micro-perspective?

If you see the world from a more global perspective and are interested in *producing* new knowledge, the right path *may* be obtaining a PhD upon completion of your PharmD. If you see the world from an individual perspective and are interested in *consuming* knowledge, you are needed on the front lines performing your clinical function no matter the setting, role, or title.

Pursuing a second doctorate was the right path for *me,* but there are things you may want to consider too. First, you will need a thirst for discovery through sound research. We have scratched only the surface of our understanding about how the social, behavioral, and economic factors affect our profession and healthcare system, and I hope to add to our understanding. Second, you should always be ready for lively debate to better understand our world and, when appropriate, challenge the assumptions of our knowledge and examine our lives. Third, I knew almost immediately why I wanted to pursue a PhD and what content areas I hoped to focus in (and you should too). My concentration in higher education administration/management was painstakingly considered as a means to best succeed in the academic environment, and better understand how to develop student pharmacists into the leaders our profession needs. Finally, having the ability to speak the language of research and practice will afford you the opportunity to be an essential team member in various professional settings or roles.

As a young practitioner, working toward the completion of a PhD has provided several rewards and posed several challenges. The knowledge obtained during a doctoral program changes the way you view the world around you, rooted in the philosophy of sound science. Your eyes are opened to how little we know about the world and how much we have conjured up in the past without evidence. While you will spend plenty of time in coursework, the conversations with colleagues, the discussions over dinners and coffee, and the students who constantly keep you sharp will provide essential developmental opportunities no text can offer. Despite this awakening, the road less traveled can be a lonely one. The responsibility of developing new knowledge takes a certain amount of rigor and diligence despite the potential for repeated failures. The importance of not losing yourself in the process cannot be overstated. Although we speak a lot about work-life balance to our colleagues and students, it is sometimes far from rewarding. The challenge of maintaining your physical, mental, and emotional well-being has to be considered.

I often ask myself why I stayed on my original residency path for so long when all the signs pointed to postgraduate completion of a PhD. As faculty, preceptors, and mentors, I often wonder if we are doing the right things for these students. Although increasing the number of student pharmacists pursuing these degree options may not be a feasible goal for pharmacy education, identifying and engaging the handful of them who have the aptitude, skills, or interest in pursuing options outside of direct patient-care roles can prove beneficial for the profession. My memories of our profession's members expressing their disappointment in me for not taking a more traditional role in pharmacy and not supporting me in my considered choices still stay with me to this day. The candid conversations I have had with students who feel bombarded by the pressure to complete residencies, despite that particular postgraduate training experience not being pertinent to their career goals, make me realize that more needs to be done to support those students. As a music lover, I would like to conclude with a lyric from the Dave Matthews Band song entitled "#41": "I will go in this way, and I will find my own way out...."

Although students and young pharmacists may begin their education as potential practitioners, they must be allowed to find their way, even if we don't understand the details of their chosen or potential career path. We must not pressure them into particular practice settings or training experiences just because we understand them better, represent them, or have greater exposure. If we allow, these rising stars can have a significant impact in our increasingly data-driven world not only through research and the potential for discovery, but also through assessment of the teaching environment due to their unique knowledge of the modern healthcare system, the medication-use process, research/statistical methods, and the biomedical sciences.

Onward and upward,

Joe

Brent I. Fox, PharmD, PhD, & Georgia W. Fox, PharmD, BCPS

Navigating the Profession and Life as a Married Pharmacist Couple: Life Will Inevitably Throw You Curveballs

Pharmacy is not only the career choice of Brent and Georgia Fox; the profession actually *brought them together*. Fifteen years later, they are a pharmacy supercouple and the parents of two young children. Like many dual-career couples, they have been faced with decisions that forced them to balance career and family demands and their mutual ambitions. The advice they share in their jointly written letter applies not only to pharmacist couples but to any dual-career couple.

Georgia W. Fox, PharmD, BCPS is in a professional staff position at Auburn University's Harrison School of Pharmacy, serving as Lead Facilitator for Integrated Pharmacotherapy, a problem-based learning course, and a mentor in the Professional Practice Experience course. She completed her PharmD degree at Auburn and completed a postgraduate year (PGY) 1 residency at Winchester Medical Center and Shenandoah University Bernard J. Dunn School of Pharmacy.

Brent I. Fox, PharmD, PhD, is Associate Professor in the Department of Health Outcomes Research and Policy at Auburn University's Harrison School of Pharmacy. He received his BS, PharmD, and PhD in Pharmaceutical Sciences at Auburn. His research focus includes pharmacy informatics education and the use of health information technology for optimal medication-related outcomes. He is co-author of two books on health informatics.

Brent and Georgia's advice is: **Life will inevitably throw you curveballs. If you have given your best every day, when unexpected events occur, you do not have to worry about your character and values being questioned.**

Dear Young Pharmacist,

We are a married pharmacy couple from Auburn, Alabama. The opportunity to share a bit of our story with today's rising stars is exciting, challenging, and humbling. It is exciting to reflect on our lives together as we pull from our experiences to provide practical advice, but it is challenging for the same reason: What useful advice can we provide? In our reflections, we were humbled by the opportunities we had and the people who supported us along the way (and continue to do so). Ultimately, we decided that the best approach is to first share how we got to where we are today, and then share the advice we wish we had been given and/or heeded. As a married pharmacy couple, the profession is certainly an important part of our daily lives. However, we are husband and wife first, so we will share professional and personal aspects of our journey together, primarily speaking to married pharmacist couples.

Our beginnings date back to 2001 when we met at Auburn University's Harrison School of Pharmacy. We dated throughout school and married a few months after graduation in 2005. In 2004, a year before graduating, Brent accepted a job at Shenandoah University in Winchester, Virginia, as an Assistant Professor and the Director of the Center for Pharmacy Informatics. Georgia followed a year later in 2005 by completing a PGY1 residency with Valley Health Systems and Shenandoah University. After a short stay in Virginia, we were fortunate to return to Auburn where we have been for the past 10 years.

Being in Virginia was a time of great personal and professional growth for both of us. This was Brent's first position after graduate school, Georgia's residency year, and our first year of marriage. Moreover, we were nearly 700 miles away from the nearest family member. We often reflect on what a great year this was for us personally because we had only each other to rely on. Professionally, we were finding our footing. Brent was learning what it meant to be a new faculty member, and Georgia was growing as a clinician.

Looking back, our time in Virginia is what laid the groundwork for who we are today. During those early days, we realized an important aspect of being married to someone in the same field—we truly understood each other's professional expectations. Brent understood the demands of a residency, and Georgia understood the demands on a new faculty member. We vividly recall supporting each other's challenges during that first year. Brent helped Georgia perfect the layout of her residency poster, served as her audience to practice class sessions, and proofread her documents. Georgia served as Brent's sounding board for new ideas to try in the classroom and helped him prepare for presentations at conferences. This mutual understanding and appreciation lightened the stress and guilt that often accompanies late night and weekend work.

When we returned to Auburn in 2006, our dynamic shifted because we both had faculty positions. Georgia accepted an Assistant Clinical Professor position, and Brent was a Visiting Professor. This was an exciting time! We had achieved our goal of returning home, even though we are not originally from Auburn. Foolishly, we anticipated that the pace of life would slow down, but we still found ourselves working late nights and weekends. Years later, we realize this is normal at the beginning of any career. It takes time to find your niche in a new setting and develop your professional network while continuing to grow your expertise. Again, we helped each other along the way; not only with the tangible tasks like developing activities and reviewing exam questions, but the intangible things like encouragement, support, and celebration after completion of a big project.

After a while, we started thinking about having a family. Although Georgia enjoyed her practice, she realized maintaining the current pace of life was not what she wanted once we had children. Auburn University underwent a curricular revision to all problem-based learning in the P3 year, which created a 9-month appointment for a Lead Facilitator. Georgia was incredibly fortunate to get this position, but it meant leaving her faculty position and earning less money. We decided this change was best for our family. This was nearly 8 years ago, and we have not regretted it for a moment.

When people find out that we are both pharmacists and work together, they frequently ask "How can you live together *and* work together?" Working together is easy, beneficial, and fun. We work in separate departments and do very different things. We do not usually see each other at work, unless we make a point to. We love that we work at the same place, especially now that we have small children. Ten minutes in the car before and after work allows a time to talk that is completely uninterrupted. Additionally, we have a better understanding of each other's responsibilities, which allows us to be more sympathetic at home and gives us the opportunity to collaborate. It also allows us to help each other say "no" and "yes" to the right things.

So, looking back over the past 10 years, what advice do we wish we had been given and what advice did we not heed?

First, we believe a supportive, professional environment is integral to successfully navigating the challenges found in both personal and professional lives. The obvious challenge to finding such an environment is determining the true nature of a professional setting. Begin by asking everyone you know who might have insight. Then, spend as much time as possible with people who are in that environment. Talk to them but also observe their interactions with others.

Our second recommendation might be the most difficult (and hokey). Determine where *home* is. Borrowing from the band Toad the Wet Sprocket, we believe that home is not where you *live*, but where you *belong*. We believe that Auburn is where we belong. We know only too well that it can be very difficult for someone to find a place they consider "home" and also find a career opportunity there.

Our point is that the sense of being grounded in the place where you belong is a powerful enabler of professional and personal growth.

Another important lesson we learned was the value of moving away from our typical support system during that first year of marriage and first professional year. The professional benefit was the opportunity to build our professional network through meeting new colleagues. This is another benefit of having a spouse in the same field; your colleagues grow exponentially. Everyone knows pharmacy is a small world. Being married to a pharmacist makes the pharmacy world even smaller. It also gave us new experiences and exposed us to new approaches in teaching, research, and clinical skills. We realize not everyone has the opportunity and/or desire to move away when starting their careers, but the option is worth considering if you do have the chance.

What if you do not find a supportive environment or the place you can call home? Well, all is not lost. Our experiences taught us the importance of married pharmacist couples supporting each other. Whatever the circumstance, use your mutual understanding of pharmacy to support each other *in the professional setting*. Although we have no quantitative data or well-controlled study, more than a decade of experience tells us shared expertise can be an asset to pharmacist couples. You have the opportunity to critically discuss professional challenges and opportunities with someone who truly understands the context. You appreciate when professional demands conflict with personal plans and provide a sounding board for new ideas. This sharing has been critical to navigating our professional lives.

We would be remiss not to mention the importance of balance. We'll start with a confession: we do not have the perfect solution. This is something we work on every day, but here are some examples of decisions we made to help us strike this balance. One of the very first decisions was Georgia's resolve to complete a residency in Virginia. We were fortunate to find a residency that matched Georgia's interests. Another decision came as a result of Brent's opportunity to serve on the Executive Committee for ASHP's Section of Pharmacy Informatics and Technology. We knew it was an opportunity he could not refuse—it would allow him to contribute professionally and provide excellent experience. However, it would mean increased travel and time away from family and his traditional job.

The secret to balance is making the best decision given all the available information. Your priorities and decisions may change as your life changes, but the process is the same every time. Know what is best for you, your spouse, family, and career; make the decision that most closely aligns. This does not mean all the decisions will be easy, and that you will not have to work hard and make concessions. If you know where you are going (for us, the goal is balance), it is easier to decide what you are willing to give and where you will stand your ground.

We also realize that we need advice. Our final recommendation to married pharmacist couples is to find one mentor who understands the profession and both individuals. This mentor should share a similar perspective on the balance between professional and personal lives. We have been fortunate to find such a colleague (a faculty member) who understands our priorities and our expectations at work but is also an invaluable source of objective advice to help us achieve our goals.

One last piece of advice before we part: work hard every moment you can. Life will inevitably throw you curveballs. We have experienced three significant ones in the past 10 years. There will come a time you will need the understanding, support, and grace of your employer and co-workers. If you have given your best every day, you do not have to worry about your character and value being questioned when these unexpected events occur.

These topics are salient to married pharmacist couples, but hopefully all readers will find value in our suggestions.

All the best,

Brent & Georgia

John B. Hertig, PharmD, MS, CPPS

Think of Your Life-Career as Your Four-Chambered Heart

John observes that as pharmacists, we often get lost in the intensity of our profession and the practice of being professional. He indicates that, although he has achieved professional successes, it was not without personal expense. Relationships suffered, and friends and quality family time were neglected. John realized with the passing of his father that a truly happy and meaningful life includes work but does not oppose it. He suggests that our lives are not unlike our four-chambered heart. We must purposefully maintain the four domains: work, home, community, and self.

John B. Hertig is currently Associate Director and Clinical Assistant Professor of Pharmacy Practice, Center for Medication Safety Advancement, Purdue University, College of Pharmacy. Previously he was Medication Safety Project Manager. He is a Certified Professional in Patient Safety (CPPS) and is serving as Director-at-Large, ASHP Section of Inpatient Care Practitioners. John received his BS and PharmD degrees from Purdue University and MS in Health-System Pharmacy Administration from The Ohio State University. John completed a postgraduate year (PGY) 1/PGY2 residency in health-system pharmacy administration at The Ohio State University Medical Center.

John's advice is: **Commit to investing in all four aspects of your life and never forget that if you adopt a singular focus on work for a prolonged period of time, you will ultimately succumb to emptiness and regret.**

Dear Young Pharmacist,

As a relatively young pharmacist, I could advise you to work hard, follow your dreams, and reach for the stars while never forgetting that you belong to one of the most storied and respected professions in the world. Although this is sound guidance, please join me as I venture in a slightly different direction. Rather than write solely about the profession of pharmacy, I will write to you about the importance of love. My closest friends and colleagues would tell you that I genuinely enjoy sharing quotes, and I often use them on the white board in my office to inspire both others and myself. As such, it is only fitting that I begin with a quote from the famous Beatle Sir Paul McCartney: "In the end, the love you take is equal to the love you make."

Take a moment to pause, recalling a fond memory that harkens to deep love. Then, put this book down and shout over to the next room or pick up the phone and call a family member, significant other, or friend and tell them you love them. Now that you have adequately expressed some love, allow me to explain why I made such an unusual request. Too often we, as pharmacists, get lost in the intensity of our profession and the state of being "professional." We forget entirely about the remaining critical parts of our lives, especially the personal ones. In the professional world, this is known as a lack of work-life balance. In my life, I have known too many people who believe that to achieve greatness we must make ruthless sacrifices, most often at the expense of our friends, family, and ourselves. I once subscribed to this flawed assumption.

When I graduated from the PharmD program at Purdue University in 2008, I struggled to maintain balance between my personal and professional lives. While I feel proud and fortunate to have achieved professional success so early on in my career, it was not without personal expense; relationships suffered, friends disappeared, and quality time with my family was neglected. This, in turn, resulted in heartache, frustration, and a general feeling that something was missing in my life. I had professional satisfaction, but I was left wanting more.

In the fall of 2014, both my life and perspective changed permanently with the sudden passing of my father. Unfortunately, many of you reading this letter have also experienced significant loss and, therefore, may understand the awakening that accompanies such a tragic event. If you have not yet experienced a personal loss, then do not wait for this to occur before changing your approach to your own life. Following the loss of my father, the fundamental change in my thinking came from the realization that my future could no longer be immersed in the constant struggle to balance work and life. The work-life balance paradigm suggests that it is work versus life; however, I now believe that a truly happy and meaningful life full of love *includes* work but does *not* oppose it.

To illustrate this concept, I want you to think of a human heart and the universally accepted symbol of life and love. As all pharmacists know, the human heart consists of four distinct chambers. Each one of these chambers must work harmoniously and be synchronized to effectively oxygenate and circulate blood throughout the body. On average, the human heart will beat approximately 2.5 billion times, representing a consistent and dedicated example of how multiple moving parts must each play a role for the entire system to thrive. Our lives are not unlike our own hearts that sustain it. Therefore, to lead a complete life—to use your whole heart—you must put forth the effort to maximize each of the following four domains in life. As described by *Harvard Business Review* writer Stew Friedman, the four chambers of your life are work, home, community, and self. Each of these areas of your own existence needs attention, monitoring, and plenty of love.

The majority of my focus was on the work chamber; I put all of my passion and energy into that one area of my life. But if one chamber of the heart is working harder than the other chambers, it causes an enlargement of that one chamber but atrophy of all others. The heart, just like our lives, is able to compensate for a defined period of time—a time during which we are able to carry on like nothing is wrong. Then suddenly, the heart begins to fail. The blood can no longer be efficiently pumped by a heart, which has been deliberately weakened by the sole focus, or rather enlargement, of the single chamber. Thus, to prevent this heart failure and to instead work on making the absolute most of our lives, we must focus on all *four* of these critical domains. We must explore our passions and professional strengths and find a way to incorporate them into our efforts at work, at home, and in our communities.

As for myself, I found success in following a nontraditional career pathway in pharmacy practice, while committing my time and resources to professional organizational involvement that allows me to impact my local community through my passion for active grassroots advocacy and legislative participation. These areas of the profession are rewarding, but they also allow me to naturally integrate my own personal interests. I recognize how fortunate I am to have mentors who help me readjust my sometimes narrowed view of pharmacy by ensuring that I focus on the "big picture" rather than professional pursuits alone.

With that said, the professional satisfaction that I have found in my career is a product of the immense impact of my mentors' guidance. In my current role as the Associate Director of the Center for Medication Safety Advancement (CMSA) and Clinical Assistant Professor of Pharmacy Practice at Purdue University College of Pharmacy, I strive to mentor others in their professional journey. I help to advance the profession by following my heart and focusing on activities that allow me to integrate my love of pharmacy with my personal interest in helping to develop people and communities. To date, this has culminated in leading a team of people, managing strategic initiatives, forming global partnerships, and educating others as an expert in medication safety. I engage in advocacy efforts nationally and locally by building on the wonderful opportunities I had as a volunteer leader and member of ASHP.

During the 2014 legislative session, with the assistance of my colleagues, I worked closely with key healthcare leaders and Indiana legislators to draft, testify, and coordinate the passage of Indiana SEA 233. This creates a pharmacy technician license while increasing the education and competency standards for pharmacy technicians throughout Indiana. Although these efforts are rewarding, this experience is a quintessential example of how, in a nontraditional professional role, I remain committed to organizational involvement and dedicated to following my personal passions. I am mindful to always give back to the profession through my organizational leadership and willingness to mentor the next generation of pharmacy dreamers.

To be professionally satisfied, you must never sacrifice your sanity for your ambition. A truly happy and meaningful life *includes* work but does *not* oppose it. Although dedication and drive to follow your passions will help ensure you achieve your dreams, it is your community, relationships, and strength in self that are critical to sustaining those dreams. If you adopt this new way of thinking, be forewarned that if you do it right you will experience failures. You will make mistakes. Perhaps you miss your child's soccer game because you had to finish work that simply could not wait. Or, maybe you decide to leave work early to celebrate an anniversary with your wife or your husband and an important email goes unsent. *That Is OK.* I have failed; you will fail; we will fail at times together. Just like the heart skips thousands and thousands of beats in a lifetime, we too will miss a beat and stumble. The key, however, is to recover by remaining committed. Never forget that if you adopt a singular focus for a prolonged period, you will ultimately succumb to a more permanent type of failure—emptiness and regret. I trust that each of you reading this letter will learn from my experience and will not make this mistake.

You will make time for friends and family. You will be the best significant other you possibly can be. You will give back to your community, place of worship, and family. You will take time for yourself to dance, cook, play, read, write, and love. You will use your pharmacy degree to improve patient care and leave the profession better than when you entered it. You will focus on all four chambers so that your heart, your passion, and your life are better than the day before. You are, or will be, pharmacists. But do not forget, you are also sons, daughters, brothers, sisters, and current or maybe future moms and dads. As for my dad, he told me he loved me during every interaction. It is one of those things that I will never forget and that I will never take for granted.

I close this letter with one more request. As you advance through your professional career, make sure that not a single day goes by without telling someone—with your own voice, as *texting* does not count—that you love him or her. Remember to focus on the four chambers of work, home, community, and self so that each may function with a synchronized purpose to allow you to create a full life. Leo Tolstoy said "Everyone thinks of changing the world, but no one thinks of changing himself." Focus on being the best self you can be by strengthening your own heart; then go ahead and, by all means, change the world.

Sincerely,

John

Felicity A. E. Homsted, PharmD, BCPS

Life Is Never What You Expect It to Be

Felicity describes how unexpected events, such as an auto accident, may alter your life and career. She shares her experiences of moving toward her ultimate goal of a leadership position and overcoming feelings of being ill prepared. Her personal involvement in becoming engaged in the political process as well as requesting a salary increase and promotion to Chief Pharmacy Officer are examples of successful efforts in getting out of your comfort zone and taking control of your life and career.

Felicity A. E. Homsted is currently Chief Pharmacy Officer and Residency Program Director, having previously been Director of Pharmacy and Residency Program Director, Penobscot Community Health Care (PCHC), Bangor, Maine. She practiced clinically as a decentralized cardiac pharmacist at Eastern Maine Medical Center in Bangor. Felicity has served as President of the Maine Society of Health-System Pharmacists and Vice Chair, Apexus Federally Qualified Health Center Advisory Council. She received her PharmD degree from Idaho State University.

Felicity's advice is: **Remember that despite our best laid plans, there are bumps in the road both literally and figuratively. How you choose to handle these setbacks will define you and your career.**

Dear Young Pharmacist,

Life is never what you expect it to be. The way you handle these bumps in the road will define you and your career. In February 2012, I was excitedly driving home after finishing my shift at the hospital. My husband and I were planning to attend the musical "Boing Boing." I noticed the lights of an approaching vehicle on an intersecting road, but I thought nothing of it because of the stop sign and ample distance between us. However, the other driver never touched his brakes. The impact sent my SUV spinning into the middle of the road, unmovable, with air bags deployed and the rear end destroyed. The other driver's full-size pickup was left looking more like an accordion. In those moments, I had no way of knowing what was to come.

When I returned to work 3 days later, I felt like I was starting over again as a new pharmacist. Everything that had come so easily to me was now a struggle. After 6 years in practice, I questioned whether 300 mg of trazadone was an appropriate dose—I had no concept of a reasonable dose for the drug. I had suffered a significant traumatic brain injury, even though I did not lose consciousness. In neuro-psychometric testing, I rated exceptional in all areas except attention and recall. In these domains, I demonstrated impairment with below average scores. My IQ placed me in the 96th percentile, but I felt like a goldfish.

Within a few months, it became clear I could not safely remain in direct patient care. The potential of a forgotten step harming someone in my care left me wondering if I could even remain in the profession. I found a part-time position as Residency Program Director at a federally qualified health center (FQHC). Initially, this job was in addition to my role as a decentralized cardiac pharmacist. I learned to slow down when working at the hospital, methodically checking and double checking to prevent mistakes. By the fall, I was hired at PCHC as a full-time Director of Pharmacy and Residency Program Director. I no longer worried about inadvertently harming my patients, but now I had a new host of challenges. None of this was easy; life rarely is.

My memory has improved somewhat thanks to donepezil, when I remember to take it. I have learned to pace myself and rely on the team approach in balancing strengths and weaknesses. Viewing setbacks and having a plan for a comeback is critical. When you get knocked down, rise back up and take the time and effort to rebuild. There is great joy in success through perseverance.

Pharmacists are detail-oriented planners. Prior to my accident, I had my entire career mapped out—bachelor's degree, doctorate, board certification, clinical specialty, manager position, MBA, and finally director. Becoming a Director of Pharmacy had been my ultimate career goal; there I was, 6 years into my career, feeling very ill prepared. Fortunately, my boss, PCHC's Chief Operating Officer, encouraged me when I questioned my readiness for the role. But there are many paths to take and more than one right answer. What is important is to have a vision for where you are going and what you want to achieve. As you are presented with opportunities, consider them in light of where you hope to end up and ask if they will help or hinder you in getting there.

Since becoming a Director of Pharmacy, my professional goals have changed. I am now working toward changing the face of pharmacy in Maine with the desire to eventually impact the nation. I believe pharmacists should be present in every primary care practice, working as integral team members to have a meaningful impact improving healthcare. In the last 4 years, this mission has led to growth in the number of PCHC pharmacists from 5 to 25 with 11 of these providing services in primacy care. What we accomplished was remarkable considering PCHC is a safety net provider with extremely limited resources, and pharmacists are non-billable providers under FQHC rules.

PCHC was selected in 2013 as a Robert Wood Johnson Exemplar Practice for Primary Care. Before heading to Seattle to meet with the other 29 recipient practices, I attended the ASHP Leadership Meeting. Still relatively new in my role, I will never forget the overwhelming sense of panic I felt sitting in a presentation where the speaker had over 25 pharmacists in the ambulatory care setting in 1984! I felt so far behind. Rationally, I was 3 in 1984, so there really was not much I could have done. Our system was insignificant compared to those I encountered at the meeting, and I left somewhat disheartened. Reaching Seattle, I interacted with primary care groups of all sizes. At the time, other groups doubted they could attain what our group had—our four pharmacists and three residents. This experience fueled my desire to create a model of primary care pharmacist integration sustainable and scalable to practices of all size, from a single physician's office to complex heath systems. As pharmacists, we have honed our skills and training and are irrefutably the medication experts. But many still see us as the pill counters. In pharmacy we spend a lot of time talking to ourselves about transforming healthcare, although others outside of our profession are unaware of our possible ties for impacting it.

My road to policy involvement was bumpy. I was desperately shy as a child, and my shyness continued into adulthood. During my first days on the cardiac floor, I had to work up the courage to call the cardiologist with questions. I constantly reminded myself that this was my job, and it was the only option. Over time it became easier. I told myself if I can effectively communicate problems to an expert who holds someone's heart in their hands and has more years of experience than I have been alive, I can handle anything. When I started advocating for pharmacist provider status, I kept this in mind!

It all started with an email from Joe Hill at ASHP. He had seen an article in *AJHP* featuring PCHC's primary care pharmacists and wanted to know if I would consider sending a letter encouraging our federal representatives to be co-sponsors in support of "Pharmacy and the Medically Underserved Enhancement Act," better known as *pharmacist provider status*. So I did what I thought any pharmacist would do—I wrote the letter. Beyond this, I drafted ones from our chief executives and enlisted staff, residents, students, colleagues, health advocacy groups, and the Maine Primary Care Association to write letters of support. Within a few days, we had one senator signed on; after many emails, visits, and discussions, our congressional representative signed too.

Working with residents and students, we ran a campaign to educate pharmacists and students about provider status and encourage advocacy. This campaign has afforded me the opportunity to meet with all members of Maine's congressional delegation representing our area. What matters most are the concerns of those you are trying to convince, their agenda, and needs—it is not about you, your profession, or your personal agenda. Understanding where you fit in that picture enables you to create a compelling case for change. At the close of each encounter, I offered my assistance in areas that they might find beneficial. Fostering relationships with people who represent you is vitally important.

Healthcare is evolving at a rapid pace. With provider status moving forward, my department growing every year, and PCHC becoming an accountable care organization (ACO), my role and responsibilities had grown significantly and my Director title no longer seemed the right fit. I was now leading a pharmacy enterprise, with four retail pharmacies and clinical services in 14 practices spanning the state as well as managing an extensive 340B program and leading medication management efforts across a 14 health-system ACO.

Through research and discussions with other colleagues, I gathered information, drafted a new job description, and arrived at my monthly meeting with PCHC's Chief Medical Officer (CMO). I guided the conversation to highlight the changes to the organization, my role, and where I hoped we were going. After reviewing positive growth and important programs, I was ready to discuss my future. "I would like my title to be changed to Chief Pharmacy Officer to reflect the role I am performing, and I would also like a raise." I threw that last part in for good measure. It was never about the money. I suggested it as a negotiation point, thinking we would agree to the title in lieu of the raise. To my pleasant surprise, the CMO said he would take this request to the CEO.

A short time later, the CEO met with me and asked why I wanted the change. I responded that it was not a change in my position but rather a more accurate reflection of the scope of my role. If I told him it was for the title or my personal recognition, I know the answer would have been "no." After talking for 2 hours, he agreed. Frankly, I was stunned—excited and stunned. If I had not asked for the promotion, it never would have happened; but, I had to earn the position before I could ask for it. Your odds of a promotion are much improved if you demonstrate that you are fully prepared for the position.

Your chances improve even more if you can show you are already doing the work. In taking a chance, being well prepared, and asking the question, I received the desired results. Always remember that even if the answer is "no," you are no further behind than you were before you asked the question. So take the chance.

Regards,

Felicity

Scott J. Knoer, PharmD, MS, FASHP

Leading an International Pharmacy Enterprise

Scott shares his leadership adventures from living/working in Germany, prior to attending pharmacy school in the Midwest, to building a common pharmacy practice vision across borders that required working successfully with different cultures. He discusses the challenge of developing cross-cultural communication skills such as hiring local pharmacy leadership talent and working in countries that have no wholesalers.

Scott J. Knoer is currently Chief Pharmacy Officer, Department of Pharmacy, Cleveland Clinic. Previously he was Director of Pharmacy, University, Riverside and Children's Hospitals, University of Minnesota Medical Center, Fairview. He received his PharmD from the University of Nebraska and his MS in Hospital Pharmacy from the University of Kansas. Scott completed a 2-year health-system pharmacy administrative residency at the University of Kansas Medical Center.

Scott advises: **Demonstrate a bias for saying yes (and do a great job on an important project), and you will be given more opportunity when it arises. Because of the response to this opportunity, you will be viewed as a "can do," action-oriented leader.**

Dear Young Pharmacist,

Long before my career in pharmacy, I lived in Germany where I worked as a Regional Manager for the British company Wedgwood that makes fine china. This position required extensive travel throughout Europe, exposing me for the first time to conducting business internationally.

Twenty-five years later, I find myself once again with international responsibilities. This time it is with operations in the United States, Canada, England, and Abu Dhabi. The experiences I had nearly forgotten from long ago came flooding back as my international footprint expanded. Those competencies include understanding the local business market as well as adapting my leadership style by demonstrating flexibility in thinking while appreciating the expertise of others.

Over the years, I have found success in applying a few universal leadership principles to doing business abroad. These critical success factors include building and leveraging key relationships, hiring the right people, delegating appropriately, planning strategically, setting goals, and ensuring accountability. To be successful across borders; however, these truths must be adapted to account for cultural norms.

Understand the local market. The most important lesson is that to best understand a local market, you must *physically* experience that setting. You have to go to the site and see things for yourself. Telephone and videoconference calls are fine for ongoing project management, but you need to meet people in person, listen to their concerns, and understand their realties to truly understand a local business environment.

For example, doing business in the Middle East is extremely complicated from a logistics perspective. Although these situations can be relayed over the phone, it isn't until you walk into a cavernous medication storage room that you truly understand it. There are no wholesalers in the Middle East. In the United States, we take for granted our ability to receive daily deliveries from our main supplier. We can order 90% of our medications from placing a single order in one computer system. In fact, we could have deliveries twice a day if we wanted to pay for it. In Abu Dhabi, due to local laws, wholesalers do not exist. Every drug company is required to use an agent to represent that product. It is not uncommon to receive a medication delivery 4 months after placing the order. These logistical challenges require hospitals to keep several months' supply to avoid running out of a medication. If we were to apply the U.S. just-in-time inventory principles to this region, we would fail miserably. Therefore, it is not logical to hold our Abi Dhabi pharmacy team to the same inventory-turn goals that we use in the United States. To be successful, the plan must be adapted to the environment.

Get the right people on board. How do you effectively manage a team across continents? The leadership principle of hiring good people and delegating with accountability becomes even more critical when working half a world away. The first and most important key to success is getting the right leader in place. To do this, you must ensure that your organization understands the importance of this leadership position and values it accordingly. If you are not financially competitive in the local market, you will get what you pay for. If you want a mediocre leader, then it is OK to operate within financial constraints that don't allow you to hire quality. If you want a top-tier leader, then you must pay competitively.

Once you have the position designed, the next step is to critically vet applicants. One thing that continues to surprise me is just how small the world really is even when working overseas. The concept of six degrees of separation (as illustrated by the "Kevin Bacon Game" phenomenon) can be applied to pharmacy, but our world is even smaller. Within two phone calls, it is likely that I will be able to find out about a person's reputation. Have they been successful? Do they develop good relationships? Do they understand the local market? Screening someone for attitude is as important as aptitude. It goes without saying that your employees abroad need to understand local laws and customs. It is equally essential that they share your vision of pharmacy practice.

I recently vetted two candidates for a potential international engagement. One was extremely prompt in replying to me and in facilitating meetings and introductions. She quickly grasped our vision for elevating practice in the region. She demonstrated aptitude through immediately articulating this vision to the rest of the consultants on our team. She was sincere in embracing this new strategy, and it showed. The other candidate spent 2 hours defending current practice in the region without attempting to understand our perspective. The decision was easy.

After a team is in place, all members should be engaged and supportive of each other. Although they are experts in the local market, you must keep them apprised of any strategic changes that impact their work. You have to be as attentive to their needs as they are to yours.

On an ongoing basis, your international team needs to be as integrated with the rest of the organization as geography and time zones allow. Include them in strategic planning sessions and in emails within the leadership team. Although not all communications will be relevant to their daily practice, they can understand what is going on back at headquarters. This perspective helps them better comprehend the challenges the entire team faces.

Life is about relationships. A leader must develop a relationship where he or she implicitly trusts their team on the ground. If you don't have this trust, then you have failed to find the right people. Assuming you have developed a relationship based on mutual trust, then you have the opportunity to both provide and receive support from afar. Nurture a relationship where your team is comfortable updating you, even when the news may be bad. This will prepare you when people outside of your department have issues that involve pharmacy because you were proactively given a "heads up."

Ongoing communication is critical. Work with the local leader to translate the enterprise pharmacy goals into ones that make sense for the local market. Have regular calls (ours are at 0800 Cleveland time, which is 1600 Abu Dhabi time) and discussions that reflect the realities on the ground. Understand that you are not the local expert. Delegate responsibility and empower your team to make decisions. Of course, as the leader, you are ultimately responsible so you need to ensure accountability too.

When I took the role of Chief Pharmacy Officer in Cleveland, I knew that we were building a hospital in the United Arab Emirates, Cleveland Clinic Abu Dhabi (CCAD). The project was a few years behind schedule but progressing well when I arrived. I met the Senior Director of Pharmacy, and we immediately hit it off as he shared my vision of transforming the practice of pharmacy in the region. He believed in the Cleveland Clinic culture and was acting as a pharmacy and patient care advocate with the goal of elevating practice.

Shortly after our initial meeting, he invited me to speak in Abu Dhabi at a Medication Safety Conference. I accepted this invitation and combined it with a site visit to the CCAD hospital that was under construction. At this conference I met another Director of Pharmacy from a medical center in Riyadh, Saudi Arabia. These directors are two of the most influential pharmacy leaders in the Middle East. Through these foundational relationships, I have been able to generate and sustain a wide network throughout the region.

Have a "bias for yes" and be a strategic opportunist. A unique international opportunity recently presented itself to our pharmacy team. We were approached to provide the personal healthcare to an international VIP (very important person). The pharmacy portion involved some international travel to set up the infrastructure from a medication perspective in all of the places this person lived and worked. I saw this as an amazing opportunity for one of our relatively young managers. Travel, excitement, and VIPs—what else could a young leader want to augment their job? Because I assumed this would be a highly desired project, I first offered it to some of our more seasoned and senior managers than our newest manager. I was surprised that the first three managers I spoke with declined, citing concerns with travel. Finally, the fourth and newest manager on the team was very excited and asked, "Where do I sign up?" He had a bias for yes and saw this as a significant opportunity.

Although I understand the need for work-life balance, I was frankly amazed that the first three team members viewed this as more of a burden than an opportunity. I would have accepted this assignment if I were them. In fact, I *did* live and work abroad at a young age.

I recently received a call from this adventurous manager who was on our VIP's personal aircraft. He was going from one country to another on a private jet to ensure that the VIP's mansions and offices had appropriate medication storage systems in place. Our manager made a lot of high-level international contacts that will inevitably be valuable later in his life. He has an international presence, which few people have at such a young age.

Now that he has demonstrated this bias for yes (and did a great job on an important project), he will be given more opportunity when it arises. His willingness to take a calculated risk paid off from both a personal development and professional advancement perspective. Because of how he responded to this opportunity, I see him as a "can do," action-oriented leader.

Finally, to be successful in any pharmacy leadership role, you need to get out of your office and go where the patients are. You need to visit every site where you have pharmacy services to understand the unique circumstances, laws, and customs.

Twenty-five years ago, I had opportunities abroad that I didn't appreciate at the time. These life experiences provided a foundation of skills that I now use as a pharmacy leader of an international health system. You develop and grow as a leader, even when you are not trying to. Pay attention to your surroundings, reflect on your experiences, and learn from the people around you.

Regards,

Scott

Paul R. Krogh, PharmD, MS, BCPS

Handling Your Personal Finances Appropriately and Other Management Advice

Paul suggests the following ways to increase your work-life balance: unplug work when it's family/personal time, think about your future and establish priorities accordingly, learn to say "no," take care of your health, ask for help, and give back to your community/profession. He also discusses making the most of your personal finances and how to be successful in leading non-pharmacy departments.

Paul R. Krogh is currently Director of Pharmacy, Respiratory Care, Interpreter Services and Infectious Diseases, North Memorial Medical Center, Robbinsdale, Minnesota. Previously he was a Pharmacy Manager, Abbott Northwestern Hospital, Minneapolis, Minnesota. He received his PharmD from the University of Minnesota and his MS in Health System Pharmacy Administration from the University of Wisconsin. Paul completed two residencies at the University of Wisconsin Hospitals and Clinics: a postgraduate year (PGY) 1 in pharmacy practice and a PGY2 in health system pharmacy administration.

Paul's advice is: **Maintain a work-life balance, invest wisely, and take advantage of your countless career path options and opportunities.**

Dear Young Pharmacist,

I appreciate the chance to share insights from what I have learned over the last 10 years, which hopefully will help you get the most out of your career. Specifically, I was asked to share my experiences regarding work-life balance, my residency training, personal finances, and oversight of departments outside of pharmacy.

Integrating work and life as you experience major personal life events. My wife and I are excited to start the next phase of our life together as parents. As a result, work-life balance is at the forefront of my mind. Like many of you, I have a demanding schedule that often requires long work days as well as some evening and weekend hours. I truly enjoy what I do, believe it is meaningful work, and am grateful for the opportunities I have been afforded through work and involvement in professional societies to advance my career and the profession. Below, I have outlined some thoughts on work-life balance:

1. **Unplug work when it's family/personal time.** Two hours of *fully* engaged time with the important people in your life is better than 4 hours of time in which you are checking your email and social media every 15 minutes. In other words, focus on optimizing the *quality* of the time versus the *amount* of time you spend with family and friends.

2. **Think about what you want your future to look like and establish your priorities accordingly.** What do you want your future to look like from both a career and family/personal perspective in 5, 10, or 15 years, and what will you need to accomplish to get there? Write down your goals as well as your current responsibilities and then place them in rank order based on what is most important to you and your family. Placing them in rank order will help ensure you are allocating your time to the most important things and also determine what you might need to let go.

3. **Learn to say "no."** When we become burned out, overwhelmed, and exhausted, we are no good to anyone including our patients, family, colleagues, and ourselves. Learning to decline requests that do not align with your priorities will help ensure that you can meet your work responsibilities and also have time for your family/personal interests.

4. **Take care of your health.** When life gets hectic, we often sacrifice ourselves for everyone and everything else. You cannot be the best partner, parent, care provider, colleague, or boss when you are unhealthy and overstressed. Schedule time to take care of yourself physically, mentally, and spiritually to ensure the best *you* is showing up every day.

5. **Ask for help.** If you are struggling to manage your current work-life schedule, don't keep it to yourself. Talk to your family, friends, colleagues, and boss to see if there is a way they can help. Asking for help isn't admitting defeat, and doing so can actually improve relationships.

6. **Take time to volunteer and give back to your community and profession.** The level of commitment you are able to give to your community and/or professional organizations will ebb and flow based on other competing priorities in your life; the personal/professional benefit you receive through volunteerism will not.

Finally, despite your best efforts, your work-life balance will get off track at times. Learn to recognize when this occurs and try to optimize your work-life balance rather than attempting to perfect it.

Administrative residency and master's program—how did they help prepare me? I am fortunate to have had two pharmacy leaders/personal mentors, Steve Kastendieck and Scott Knoer, who encouraged me to pursue a 2-year administrative residency and Master's program after my rotations with them in my final year of pharmacy school. I can unequivocally say this was the best career advice I have ever received! I spent the following 2 years completing the administrative residency program and obtaining a Master's degree at the University of Wisconsin Hospital and Clinics/University of Wisconsin–Madison. I had the opportunity to work and learn from pharmacists on the front line, with supervisors and managers in every aspect of pharmacy, and also with leaders and departments outside of pharmacy. The wide range of experiential and didactic experiences inside and outside of the pharmacy profession, the rigorous schedule of being a resident as well as a full-time student, and the dedication and support of my preceptors and mentors provided me with the knowledge and confidence to take on a challenging leadership position post-graduation. In addition, I left Madison with not only a new set of skills and experiences, but also with lifelong friends from my residency class and a network of pharmacy leaders who I continue to rely on for support and knowledge.

Financial recommendations. You are entering a profession that is both professionally and financially rewarding. Early in your career, you should pursue the following to establish yourself and family (if applicable) for a comfortable and sustainable lifestyle and retirement:

1. **Find a trusted financial advisor**. When selecting a financial planner, look for someone who is a Certified Financial Planner (CFP) and verify his or her credentials. Consider the plans' payment structure. Some financial planners are paid on commission for buying and selling stock or other items such as supplemental life insurance plans. Others are paid a flat fee or percent of annual assets for their counsel and do not get a cut from life insurance or fund companies. In general, a financial planner with a set annual fee is preferable; it avoids pressure to invest in certain insurance and/or mutual funds packages because the CFP gets no cut of that revenue. Finally, check with other friends and/or colleagues to see if they have any recommendations.

2. **Develop a long-term retirement plan**. Determine how you want to enjoy your post-career life and then create an investment strategy that will provide you the retirement income to do so. Your financial advisor can help you create your retirement roadmap.

3. **Max out your company's matching program**. Most employers will match your investment in their 401(k) retirement program up to a certain percentage, which is essentially free money for you. Contributions to a 401(k) plan will also help lower your taxable income, and the money that grows in the account is tax-deferred.

4. **Get your student loans under control and pay them on time**. If you are considering refinancing your student loans, look for a low interest rate and also a "no pre-pay penalty" option to provide the ability to pay off your loans sooner if it makes financial sense to do so.

5. **Save money**. Try and save 10-15% of your income each year and up to 3 months' earnings for emergencies or investment opportunities.

6. **Review your 401(k) plan's performance every year**. Your goal is to keep pace with the market. In general, most financial advisors consider 5-8% growth rate a good return. If your investment portfolio is experiencing large positive or negative swings from year to year, work with your financial advisor to evaluate the allocations. To decide how much of your investments to have in stocks versus bonds, subtract your age from 100. The number that remains is the percentage of your investments that is recommended to be invested in stocks. Many retirement plans have "set it and forget it" investment strategies, which are designed to automatically adjust your investments more heavily in stocks earlier in your career and then transition to lower risk bonds as you move closer to retirement.

7. **Purchase life insurance to cover your student loans, mortgage (if applicable), and four to eight times your annual salary**. Most employee-sponsored plans allow you to buy an additional four to six times your salary in supplemental coverage over and above what's provided as the base coverage plan. Your financial advisor may recommend additional supplemental life insurance above and beyond your employee-sponsored plan depending on other financial/personal factors.

8. **Consider purchasing supplemental long-term disability insurance**. Many employers provide group long-term disability benefits that will pay you a portion, often 55-65% of your base salary, should you become disabled. If you determine you need to cover a higher percentage of your salary to meet financial obligations and/or maintain your current lifestyle, consider bridging the gap by supplementing your employer-sponsored coverage with individual disability insurance.

Overseeing departments outside of pharmacy. About 18 months ago, my leadership role expanded when the Respiratory Care and Interpreter Services departments were moved under my direction. My responsibilities further expanded to include the Infectious Diseases service line as we transitioned to employed, rather than contracted, infectious disease providers. I am discovering numerous opportunities, challenges, and risks in taking on this expanded organizational role outside of pharmacy. These new responsibilities have provided opportunities to develop and strengthen relationships with other organization colleagues and leaders. For example, working as dyad partners with the departments' medical directors has increased my visibility and influence with our medical staff.

Gaining an understanding of the current state, opportunities, and challenges facing the team members in a different department—outside of my professional training—definitely has involved a steep learning curve. I was particularly concerned when I took over our Interpreter Services department. I was fortunate to have had organizational support to bring in external consultants to provide a baseline assessment of the department's performance, compliance with legal and regulatory requirements, and opportunities to better serve our non-English speaking patient population. This was a valuable exercise and provided the background to create a long-term strategy for the department.

Although my expanded role has resulted in less time available to focus on pharmacy-specific initiatives, it has provided the opportunity to view how pharmacy services can best support our patients and organization from different perspectives.

In closing, you have chosen a career that has countless career path options and opportunities; take advantage of it! Wherever your career takes you, approach each opportunity with passion and enthusiasm—carpe diem!

Sincerely,

Paul

Ashley E. Lanham, PharmD, MBA

Whatever Is Worth Doing at All Is Worth Doing Well

Like many of us, a role model inspired Ashley to become a pharmacist. In Ashley's case, this role model was her grandfather who practiced pharmacy in his small-town community pharmacy with compassion and enthusiasm. Ashley's other inspiration, which helped her survive the rigorous academic challenges of a dual degree, came as advice from a wise teacher.

Ashley E. Lanham is currently Program Manager - Quality Network Clinical Pharmacist at Humana. Prior to joining Humana, she served as Manager of Student Development and New Practitioner Programs at the Academy of Managed Care Pharmacy (AMCP) and completed the Executive Fellowship at the National Association of Chain Drug Stores (NACDS) Foundation. A native of Kentucky, Ashley received her PharmD from the University of Kentucky College of Pharmacy and her MBA from the Gatton College of Business and Economics at the University of Kentucky. She is an active member of AMCP, ASHP, the American Pharmacists Association, and the American Society of Association Executives.

Ashley's advice is: **Remember my teacher's meaningful message that has inspired me to work hard and pursue my dreams—whatever is worth doing at all is worth doing well.**

Dear Young Pharmacist,

Congratulations on choosing a wonderful and rewarding career in pharmacy! You will be amazed at the many career opportunities available to you and the positive impact you can have on patients' lives. I am so honored to be writing this letter, and I hope my experiences and advice will be beneficial.

For as long as I can remember, I wanted to be a pharmacist. I grew up in a small Kentucky town with fewer than 1,000 people. My grandfather was the local pharmacist and independent pharmacy owner. (Although he has sold the pharmacy, he still practices at age 73 and loves every minute of it). I was raised in that pharmacy and watched my grandfather treat his patients like family. I saw the passion he had (and still has) for his practice, and I wanted the same for my future. I had my first job dusting shelves in that pharmacy, and then I served as a pharmacy technician. My grandfather's work ethic and compassion still inspire me today. I'm so lucky to have him as a mentor. I hope that you are fortunate enough to have a great mentor in your life who inspires you to be a better pharmacist and person.

I want to share with you a story and a motto I carry with me daily. I learned from many great teachers and educators throughout my life, but one stands out in my mind. Mr. Montgomery taught me math, history, and religion throughout middle school and high school. He was a challenging teacher, pushing students to the next level. He always gave a pep talk at the beginning of each semester, and I remember the first one in particular. He wrote a quote in big red letters on the bulletin board in the front of the classroom: "Whatever is worth doing at all is worth doing well." He spoke about the importance of taking pride in your work and being confident in your answers. This lecture and quote has stuck with me throughout my personal and professional life. I hope that you will think about this story the next time you have a challenging patient or project and remember the importance of taking pride in your practice.

By heeding this advice and putting 100% effort into my school work, I was recognized by my pharmacy school peers and professors for my diligence and persistence. Growing up in an independent community pharmacy, I always enjoyed learning about the business side of pharmacy—patient satisfaction, finances, etc. My interest in business led me to apply to the University of Kentucky College of Pharmacy where they offer a PharmD/MBA dual degree program. After starting this program, I realized I wanted to pursue a nontraditional pharmacy career path—something much different than my independent pharmacy upbringing. I wanted to find a career where I could use my pharmacy and business knowledge beyond the direct patient care level and toward the broader healthcare landscape. The dual degree program was a huge commitment, requiring up to 26 credit hours for some semesters. This was challenging at times, but the combination of pharmacy and business intrigued me. In the end, the dual degree set me apart from many student pharmacists applying for the same positions.

Aside from the demands of the dual degree, leadership development and soft skills were also important to me. I sought out every opportunity to be a leader in my class and in the college. Many of the skills I learned as a chapter president directly transfer to my current role in managed care and previous roles in association management—managing meetings, working with committees, and managing relationships/members. By no means was I the only student pharmacist with such lofty goals and a large course load. I was intimidated by all these like-minded individuals at first. I had completed only 2 years of undergraduate work at fairly small universities in small-class settings before attending pharmacy school. In pharmacy school, it felt like everyone was living by my motto. This is where I really learned the value of relationship building. We all had 4 years of pharmacy school to meet our goals and be the best version of ourselves at graduation. Being supportive of my classmates' goals and helping them achieve success was a great experience and gift to me. We were all living my motto by supporting each other.

After deciding to pursue a nontraditional career path, I positioned myself to learn as much as possible about these roles before graduation and the associated postgraduate training opportunities. I started with job shadowing and then set up my rotations to gain as much exposure as possible. I even took an extra rotation in the place of my off-rotation to experience another practice setting. During the job interview process, I had narrowed my interests to association management and pharmaceutical industry fellowships. In the end, it was my rotation at NACDS that led me to pursue the NACDS Foundation Executive Fellowship.

Early in my career, I learned association management was my passion and fit in well with the business skills I had gained in my education. The NACDS Foundation Executive Fellowship, a nontraditional postgraduate training program, taught me the basic operations of an association. The 1-year program also vastly expanded my network all across the pharmacy world, including a connection that led to my next role in association management at AMCP. In that position, I worked with pharmacists and student pharmacists across the country. To me, the two most attractive aspects of association management are working with colleagues across the practice continuum and having a real impact on our profession. After starting my career in association management, my time at the NACDS Foundation and AMCP led me to pursue a career at Humana where my role allows me to work with a number of stakeholders to improve quality of care while reducing costs. My days are never the same, making every day especially exciting. I challenge you to think about your passion and what career path will enable you to ignite it.

I have had some struggles along the way, including confidence issues. Although I was really involved in student pharmacist organizations and a student leader at college, I still didn't feel confident. Through practice and feedback from my colleagues and mentors, I feel much more confident today. Yes, I still get nervous during public speaking engagements; but if you ask those close to me, they would say my public speaking skills have improved tenfold through practice and delivering my message with more confidence. Public speaking is something we all have to do at some point, whether it is at a pharmacy meeting or at a local community meeting. l will continue to work hard to improve my public speaking skills because I believe that you should put forth your best effort.

Remember, you bring a unique background and set of experiences to your practice—something different from every other pharmacist. Capitalize on your experiences and be the best pharmacist for your patients. It is common, especially when we are applying for the same residencies and fellowships, to compare ourselves to others—but we should not. When I was applying for postgraduate training opportunities, I remember thinking I needed to have the longest CV or the best cover letter. I was wrong. I just needed the best version of me to represent my work and set of experiences.

Whenever you are feeling challenged, always remember my motto "whatever is worth doing at all is worth doing well."

Best of luck in your career!

Ashley

Matthew (Matt) Lennertz, PharmD, MS

Sometimes the Ideal Opportunities Are Disguised in the Disappointment of Missing Out on Another Opportunity

Matt readily admits that he has more experience in hockey than in pharmacy. But that has not stood in the way of his star rising in pharmacy. In fact, it was a quote from a legendary hockey coach that provided the impetus for Matt to pursue—and excel in—his chosen career path of managed care pharmacy. Matt describes how setbacks and disappointments in his career later opened up even better opportunities.

Matthew (Matt) Lennertz is currently Director of Pharmacy Innovation and Analytics at Gateway Health. His previous experience includes serving as Clinical Project Manager at Magellan Health and Clinical Pharmacist at Healthspring. Matt received his PharmD at Temple University and his MS in Pharmaceutical Outcomes and Policy at the University of Florida. He completed a managed care pharmacy residency at Walgreens Health Initiatives. He is an active member and volunteer in the Academy of Managed Care Pharmacy (AMCP).

His advice is: **Seize opportunities, work hard, be open to new possibilities when things don't turn out as you hoped, and, of course, listen to the hockey coach.**

Dear Young Pharmacist,

Considering I have played ice hockey since I was 5 years old and have been a pharmacist for only 7 years, I have more experience in hockey than pharmacy.

Sound advice can come from all areas of life and a quote from the 1980 U.S. Olympic Ice Hockey Coach, Herb Brooks, particularly impressed me. Before the 1980 U.S. Olympic ice hockey team beat the Russians in the biggest upset in sports history, Brooks said "Great moments are born from great opportunity, and that is what you have here tonight, boys. That's what you have earned here tonight."

Two aspects of this quote have guided me throughout my life and pharmacy career: you have to *earn* your opportunities, and you have to *recognize* the opportunity in every situation to take advantage of it. Opportunities are earned through bold action and hard work, differentiating you from your peers. Recognize opportunities in every situation because they won't always seem ideal at the time and may arise out of disappointment. Without following these two principles, I would not have advanced to where I am in my career.

If I hadn't recognized an opportunity while in pharmacy school, I would still be working at the same pharmacy chain where I was an intern. In my third year of pharmacy school, I completed a self-study research project instead of taking an elective. I didn't think much of the opportunity—completing a project focused on prior authorization rates in retail pharmacies at the time and learning about managed care pharmacy principles, which were not stressed in school. Although I look back on the project now as the work of a naive student, it was published in a journal with assistance from my faculty advisor. The project and subsequent publication created many opportunities and led me down a different career path.

The new career path was managed care pharmacy. I was intrigued by the population health aspects of managed care and the large impact a pharmacist can have in that setting. I appreciated the individual patient interaction and intervention to improve health through counseling and increasing medication adherence in a retail setting. However, I was more interested in the impact that a program (e.g., adherence initiative in a managed care setting) could have on improving the health of thousands of patients. I also appreciated the challenge in managed care in striving not only to provide the most effective therapy, but also in being the least costly therapy to ensure healthcare affordability.

For pharmacists who are interested in population health and health economics, I recommend researching managed care pharmacy careers and especially through AMCP. I wanted to pursue a career in managed care pharmacy after doing my research; I worried about being too late because students at other schools had been involved in AMCP chapters since the beginning of pharmacy school. I was at a disadvantage compared to them but decided to take bold action to create an opportunity. Although I didn't receive a managed care experiential rotation, I approached the person in charge and was able to leverage the fact that I was very interested in one into a experiential rotation at a PBM. The bold action was taking charge by trying to obtain the experiential rotation after I initially did not receive it.

Following my practical experience on my rotation, I realized the best way to earn a position in a managed care company would be completing a managed care residency. I also realized that bold action would be needed yet again because I found myself competing with others who had been preparing for a residency throughout pharmacy school. I hoped my somewhat unimpressive resume would be bolstered with my published paper, my managed care rotation, and my research through AMCP. After I interviewed for several managed care residencies around the country, my first choice was a residency at the PBM in the Philadelphia area where I had completed my rotation and lived most of my life. Initially I considered listing only the one residency that wouldn't require moving to a new city, but decided I had to seriously consider moving for a residency. I ended up matching to a residency at a PBM in Chicago. It was disappointing at first, because the idea of moving to a new city (where I didn't know anyone) was daunting. However, in hindsight, it turned out to be an amazing opportunity. If you have to move for a residency, think of it as a 1-year commitment to personal and professional growth by stepping out of your comfort zone. The daring action of moving to a new city and taking advantage of an opportunity that didn't seem ideal advanced my career.

At the end of my residency, I applied to many positions but never made it past the interview stage. So I returned to the Philadelphia area to work as an overnight floater pharmacist for the same chain where I worked while in school. After about a month of overnight shifts and applying to many positions, a health plan in Nashville offered me a position. Again, I had to move to another city to pursue my goal. My advice from this experience is: take advantage of the first offer, even though it won't seem ideal and is not your first choice. Completing a residency does not entitle you to a position, and your first position afterward will probably be entry level. Remember that your first position allows you to get "your foot in the door." Everyone needs to start somewhere, and the experience you gain will pay dividends for the rest of your career.

For several years, I worked for that company; it was the perfect first job. I learned about many different areas, including clinical criteria and formulary development. After a few years, another opportunity came about through an acquisition of another health plan in Baltimore. I moved in the hope of getting a manager position but was disappointed when I didn't receive it. However, my disappointment did not last long—I was offered a manager position a short time later with a different company.

Bold actions, a solid reputation, and making a good impression are all essential in earning opportunities, which led me to my current role. The managed care pharmacy world is a small place; if you pursue this type of career, you will probably work with many of the same people throughout your career. Early in my new position, a supervisor two levels above my position noted my hard work and continued dedication to differentiating myself by pursing a Master's degree focused on pharmacoeconomics. The supervisor subsequently left that company but, in the small world of managed care pharmacy, hired me for a director position when I applied for a job at her new employer. So, my hard work and reputation at one company earned me a director position leading a team of pharmacists and analysts at a new company.

If you remember anything from my letter to apply to your life or pharmacy career, it should be twofold. *First,* you need to earn opportunities through working hard, maintaining an excellent reputation, and not being afraid to step out of your comfort zone. *Second,* grab opportunities when they present themselves, even if they are not your first choice. Sometimes the ideal opportunities are disguised in the disappointment of missing out on another, so recognize the potential in every situation.

Sincerely,

Matt

Robert (Rob) A. Lucas, PharmD, MBA, BCPS, FASHP

The Impact of Succession Planning and Paving the Way for Others

Rob didn't know how valuable mentors could be until he realized *they* saw his potential before *he* did. After graduating from pharmacy school, Rob saw himself just trying to get a job where he could be useful as a clinical pharmacist and never considered he might be a director of pharmacy. This dramatic career shift resulted from a succession plan, which his retiring director put in place. She suggested that he participate in the ASHP Foundation's Pharmacy Leadership Academy and then use the credits to complete an MBA, which has made all the difference in his career.

Robert (Rob) A. Lucas is currently Director of Pharmacy. Previously, he was Pharmacy Clinical Coordinator at Blount Memorial Hospital in Maryville, Tennessee. He received his PharmD from Samford University and his MBA in Healthcare Management from New England College. Rob completed a pharmacy practice residency at Saint Thomas Hospital, Nashville, Tennessee.

Rob's advice is: *If you are trying to inspire individuals who are not satisfied in their roles but not practicing at the top of their abilities, never give up on them and treat them with respect.*

Dear Young Pharmacist,

Not long ago, I graduated from pharmacy school with my sights set on being a pharmacist in a hospital. But my career has taken several twists and turns, and my daily activities are not what I expected.

In my first position as a pharmacist, the Director of Pharmacy did not see much potential in me. However, the Clinical Coordinator did; I gravitated to him, worked hard, and earned additional duties. I didn't realize how useful that first mentor would become. I recall those experiences and advice when making decisions today; keep this in mind as you consider working more closely with someone who is seasoned and decides to invest in you. Observe the work they are doing and volunteer to help by taking tasks from them that *you* can accomplish. Get to know how they think and get to know them as a person. Over time, they will lean on you and provide opportunities for your growth. More responsibility leads to more job satisfaction, which tickles that reward center in your professional life.

After almost 6 years at my first position, I accepted a job 3 hours away at a smaller hospital for a seemingly lateral career move. After 5 months, my supervisor (also our Director of Pharmacy) asked me to accompany her to the Tennessee Pharmacists Association leadership retreat. I saw her network and participate in policy-making decisions; I, too, was able to network and make new acquaintances across the state. I did not realize until the end of the meeting that my boss was actually the President of the Tennessee Society of Health-System Pharmacists (TSHP). That weekend opened my eyes to a whole new world and set the stage for my professional metamorphosis.

Eventually, my supervisor suggested I replace her upon retirement and asked me to work with her on succession planning. I never considered being responsible for a whole department. She suggested that I attend a newly developed ASHP program called the Pharmacy Leadership Academy. Initially, I thought the program would entail copious amounts of work outside of my job, leaving little time for my wife (also a full-time pharmacist), three kids, and triathlon training. I followed her advice and started the Academy in January 2012. Meanwhile, I was promoted into a new job as Pharmacy Clinical Coordinator, and the tools I learned in the Academy helped me immensely with strategic planning and working with a new Chief Financial Officer (CFO) on financial aspects of the pharmacy. As the Clinical Coordinator, I was leading and guiding the vision and efforts of the residency program, decentralized clinical pharmacists, and the central pharmacy. The Academy was instrumental in providing basics on dealing with personnel matters of leadership as well as departmental challenges. My Director had a vision based on 30+ years of experience, but I didn't see it. So when a proven leader gives you advice, you should listen. Sometimes you don't know what you don't know.

Do you ever feel that after working so hard to get through pharmacy school (or residency) you just want to coast for a while? I finished the Leadership Academy 2 months after my fourth child was born and then immediately enrolled in a MBA program for healthcare. Even though it was going to be a financial burden, I figured that I would be working for 25-30 more years. I needed to support four children and two weddings (I have two daughters); and I could use the extra skills for dealing with a changing healthcare landscape. I completed the Academy training and MBA, and now have wealth of experience, which I rely on every day! Two months after graduating from the MBA program, I worked with the CFO to find out why our pharmacy was $500,000 over budget. I actually used the tools and skills learned from the Master's program. Four years ago, these tasks would have seemed daunting, but it was fairly simple thanks to my MBA experience. The financial knowledge I gained has been used not only at work but also at home with personal finances.

My leadership experience now includes being a retired U.S. Army Officer, Past President of TSHP, chair of multiple committees, and involvement with the ASHP Commission on Affiliate Relations. But no matter what position you are in, you can lead those around you. You can become an informal leader within your current environment. Begin by investing in someone else. Mentor a technician or student. From my supervisor and the Academy, I learned to be the example I want my leaders to be.

One of my toughest leadership challenges is trying to inspire individuals who are not satisfied in their roles and who are not practicing at the top of their abilities. The Academy taught me to find the talents of each individual and match it with responsibility. I learned never to give up on people and to treat them with respect. Merely sharing your personal experiences may help other pharmacists struggle less.

I hear newer graduates say they could succeed without taking on extra studies or responsibilities, or that they don't have extra time. Investing your time and money in yourself and in the profession will pay big dividends. It will create not only a better work environment, but also position you to have a better work schedule for your family time. The cumulative effect of investing in your professional life with time and money will show in your confidence, fulfillment, and job security, which leads to greater happiness. So take the extra steps beyond the basic required continuing education (CE) and, after a while, you will find what you like and where your talents lie.

Why on earth would you want to take a board certification exam that costs $600 and does not ensure a raise or extra benefits at work? About 7 years ago, when I had been out of school for 11 years, I took the Board Certified Pharmacotherapy Specialist (BCPS) exam. I have since realized further benefits of certification. For BCPS CE, I download and read recent articles at my leisure and answer 20-30 questions online. I use the articles to keep up-to-date, get CE credits, and share them with my students and residents. It helps me feel like I'm not falling behind. Because all pharmacists must complete CE credits, why not do a little extra and achieve some recognition for obtaining and maintaining knowledge that is used in patient care?

Have you ever thought about serving on a committee in your state or national organization? Do you wonder what they do, how much time it takes, or what you would get out of it? In potential new residents and new pharmacists to hire, I look for membership in state and national pharmacy societies. You might think that the membership fees are too high or that you don't know how to get involved. I believe that you can't afford *not* to be member. The fees are only a fraction of your annual salary but can pay big dividends in ways you might not realize. Participating in a committee takes only a couple of hours per year, usually through a conference call or two, and it's not as complicated as you might think. The first committee I served on was the awards committee, and I didn't say a word on the conference calls. I simply listened, and I absorbed it all. When you learn what others across the country are doing, you'll have more ideas to use where you work.

Many pharmacists want to find a balance between family life and taking on more professional responsibilities. Choosing no more than three professional goals per year would get you to a comfort level where you can be involved but also have ample time for your personal life. You can make life easier at work, too. Plenty of information is available in publications, journals, newsletters, and list-serves. I learned how to tap into it without feeling overwhelmed and to do it at my own pace. During the week, I keep up with the literature by reviewing information sent to me through emails, such as with listserve postings, and choose to either delete the emails or use them to help my pharmacy. I also try to read about three books per year on different topics that are not necessarily for pharmacists or even health-care related. Examples are books on finance, finding your talents, leadership, faith, or even trends.

Prior to participating in any serious conversation or meeting, read through all of the materials to be discussed, brush up on subjects, print pertinent articles, and write down top five items that you think should be considered. You will have a rewarding experience and contribute more, and you will also garner the respect of others around you.

Even if you don't like your current job responsibilities, perform at your highest level because your experiences and the reputation you earn will be beneficial later in your career. Straight out of residency, I worked as an I.V. Room Pharmacist and an Operating Room Pharmacist for over 3 years. Now, I use that knowledge as I collaborate with other departments in the hospital. Work that seems like a distraction or is unsatisfying may actually provide a strong, well-rounded foundation for your future.

When I graduated from pharmacy school, I saw myself as just trying to get a job where I could be useful as a clinical pharmacist and never thought that I would be taking a position as a Director of Pharmacy. I moved into that position this year. I love my responsibilities and look forward to going to work every day. Your dream job can become a reality, too, *if* you put in the extra effort to make it happen. Anything is possible.

Sincerely,

Rob

Marni Lun, PharmD, MBA

Tapping into the Influence of a Few to Positively Impact the Actions of Many

In her quest to find the pharmacy role that ignited her passion and fulfilled her goals, Marni pursued a career in the pharmaceutical industry, focusing on disease areas where her expertise could have a positive impact on patients. Along the way, she became an expert in identifying and developing relationships with healthcare opinion leaders and later collaborating with professional associations. This work helped her not only develop an appreciation for the value of expert opinion, thought leadership, and collaboration, it also helped her realize the importance of developing well-informed opinions.

Marni Lun is currently Director of Professional Association Relations at Novo Nordisk, Inc. Before joining Novo Nordisk, Marni was Director of Member Relations for the Pharmacy Student Forum at ASHP. An avid Florida Gator fan, she earned her PharmD and MBA degrees at the University of Florida. She is an active member of the Obesity Medicine Association, The Obesity Society, Obesity Action Coalition, American Association of Clinical Endocrinologists, and ASHP.

Marni's advice is: **Marry your well-researched thoughts with your opinions and use your confidence in your well-informed opinions to positively influence others.**

Dear Young Pharmacist,

Professional leaders are among us every day—at your university, your pharmacy, your state or national association, and elsewhere. Leaders come in many varieties, but a few emerge to positions where they can effectively influence the thoughts, opinions, and actions of others. Even fewer are able to shape the profession or healthcare in our country and world. There is a term to describe these individuals: *thought leaders* or *opinion leaders*. Do you know one? Do you want to *be* one?

The fact that you are reading this letter is promising. I encourage you to make a habit of seeking out and supporting those among us who can inspire and guide our profession to a place of greatness. Even better, I encourage you to continue on the path to becoming a thought and opinion leader yourself. We need you. But, it's tough. I think President John F. Kennedy got it right when he said "Too often we enjoy the comfort of opinion without the discomfort of thought."

With so much going on in our world, our nation, and our profession, it is impossible to be an expert on everything. Thus, we rely on the thoughts and opinions of trusted experts to guide the way. This makes sense! But, do not be too quick to accept opinions handed down to you without employing your own thoughts and perspectives to qualify them and to shape your views.

So, why have I chosen to write a letter about thought and opinion leadership? Let me explain. I knew fairly early in my pharmacy school education that my career would not likely take a traditional path. It became obvious to me that I would need to make a choice. Did I want to know a little about everything in pharmacy or a lot about one certain area? I found that, for me, being a generalist would not lead me in a direction of career satisfaction. Thus, I opted for expertise. My biggest dilemma was not knowing what specific area of pharmacy I wanted to pursue. The options were vast. I felt a little lost, a little confused, and a little excited about the possibilities. Despite the ambiguity, I liked the idea of becoming a pharmacist. The knowledge I would acquire and the influence I could have to promote the well-being of others provided my motivation to persevere through a 4-year pharmacy program and a 2-year business program.

With the opinions and suggestions of some pharmacy greats who came before me, I opted to start my career in the pharmaceutical industry. I landed a fellowship position supporting a large, field-based medical team focused on bone health and osteoporosis. We worked with experts and opinion leaders who were shaping the practice of medicine. From there I moved into a healthcare professional marketing role, this time in gastrointestinal health and ulcerative colitis. Within a few years, the infamous "volatility" of industry jobs hit home, and I had to make a major career choice. I exited the industry and pursued a different type of thought leader engagement—this time at ASHP. I had the privilege of working with the best of the best when it came to student leaders in pharmacy, many of whom were already on their way to having great influence on our profession. After ASHP, I took a position back in industry dedicated to identifying and cultivating relationships with the top national opinion leaders in the field of diabetes care. I have now landed in a role where I focus on collaboration with professional associations that have the potential for the greatest impact in the medical management of obesity. All were very different roles, but all had a similar thread tying them together—tapping into the influence of a *few* to positively impact the actions of *many*.

By some stroke of luck and through a series of rather unpredictable twists and turns, I developed into an expert of sorts on opinion makers and thought leaders in the field of medicine and pharmacy. I have learned how to identify them, build a relationship with them, and skillfully uncover areas of mutual interest for collaboration and partnership. I have the fortune of knowing and working with leaders in medicine and pharmacy who masterfully blend their expert thoughts and opinions to shape the practice of healthcare in our world. After graduating from pharmacy school at the University of Florida just a decade ago, I was blissfully unaware of the journey ahead of me that would lead to such a fulfilling role in our profession.

Okay, enough about me! This is America. In America, everyone is entitled to an opinion. It is not hard to come by a diverse set of strong opinions on any given topic in our society. Not all opinions are of equal value. It is safe to say many opinions lack significant thought, adequate expertise, and sufficient wisdom. Here is the problem we face when it comes to opinion leadership in healthcare—we must be careful who we classify as an expert before accepting their opinion as our own. It has taken me over a decade to hone this skill, and I still falter. But I keep trying. I try to seek out the best and the brightest. Not just the most intelligent, but those with the highest level of integrity and passion to improve the lives of others. I try to learn from them, support them, collaborate with them, and hopefully become more like them.

I repeat, not all opinions are equal. I have learned this from experience and continue to be astounded (both in positive and negative ways) by the influence that opinions can have on the practice of medicine and pharmacy. *My advice:* be mindful of who you allow to influence your thoughts and opinions.

If you are still interested in tapping into the wealth of knowledge and wisdom from thought and opinion leaders or if you are interested in one day becoming one, consider the following:

1. **Get to know those who are influencing your decisions.** Read faculty bios! Grab a coffee with a professor or a lecturer whenever possible and conduct a mini-interview to learn about their journey. Walk away with a better understanding of what has shaped their opinion.

2. **Decide what attributes you find most important to qualify someone as an expert worthy of influencing your thoughts and opinions.** Is it years of experience? Academic accomplishment? There are many contributors to knowledge and expertise.

3. **Don't be afraid to entertain a thought or opinion.** Noodle it around in your mind as long as necessary before accepting or rejecting it.

4. **Allow yourself to be wrong. Allow yourself to be right. Allow yourself to accept the gray zone between wrong and right.** Seek the expertise, thoughts, and opinions of many to help shape your view and move you out of the gray zone.

5. **Resist the urge to be permanently neutral.** Have a genuine thought and an opinion on important issues. Just make sure you seek out the best knowledge to support your choice, and always leave the door open for new information to inform and influence your stance.

6. **Be transparent.** Be able to share with others what has shaped your opinion.

7. **Listen to all sides of an argument.** Listen to *hear*, not to *respond*. Seek out a contrary opinion. Two credible experts can have divergent opinions and thoughts on the same subject. Take it all in! Debate it among your peers and develop a deeper understanding and appreciation for the issue at hand.

8. **Start small and practice your way to thought and opinion leadership.** If you can identify a small challenge or problem in your current workplace or institution, take it upon yourself to become the local expert on how to address the issue. Then take steps to enact change:
   - Propose a solution.
   - Demonstrate, measure/quantify, and document improvement.
   - Get buy-in from peers and management.
   - Share your knowledge with other departments or institutions.

Most importantly, marry your well-researched thoughts with your opinions. Use your confidence in your well-informed opinions to positively influence others.

Move our profession forward!

Marni

Lesley R. Maloney, PharmD

Everyone Loves a Good Story

Lesley learned very early in her career that a good story can be the key to having your message received. She describes how she used real-life stories and analogies to make her case, even using her experience shopping for a dining room table to set herself apart from other residency applicants.

Crafting a compelling and clear story is even more critical to Lesley R. Maloney in her current role as Senior Policy Advisor in the Office of the Commissioner of the U.S. Food and Drug Administration (FDA). In this role she leads, develops, and coordinates public health regulatory policy for drugs, biologics, devices, and other public health issues. Lesley joined FDA in 2010 as an Industry Liaison in the Commissioner's Office, holding several progressively responsible positions, including Deputy Associate Commissioner for External Affairs and Deputy Chief of Staff. Lesley received her PharmD degree from the University of Oklahoma College of Pharmacy and completed the ASHP Executive Residency in Association Management and Leadership. Before joining FDA, she worked in the pharmaceutical industry, at a quality improvement organization on Medicare Part D, and at a professional pharmacy association.

Lesley's advice is: **One of the most important stories you need to develop is your own. Everyone loves a good story, so be intentional about making yours great.**

Dear Young Pharmacist,

Everyone loves a good story. Whether you are sitting on the back porch with family, around a campfire with friends, or in the break room with work colleagues, stories provide a way for us to inspire, to educate, to remember, or to connect. I can't claim to be the kind of person who keeps people on the edge of their seats or doubled over in laughter. But, like a comedian rehearsing a joke in different clubs until he perfects the punchline, I recognize the value in carefully crafting a message to optimize the impact on the audience. And now in my role as a Senior Policy Advisor in the Commissioner's Office at FDA, I construct "stories" to help the Agency identify and implement workable solutions to complex policy challenges.

My first lesson in professional storytelling occurred during college, when I worked as a small-town bank teller on the weekends. To streamline operations, the bank's policy was to shut down its internal computer network each Friday at closing time and reopen the network on Monday. Unfortunately, that policy resulted in weekend tellers, like me, providing only limited services to customers. It also meant our data lagged a day or two behind. In addition to being inconvenient for tellers, I thought the policy didn't meet our mission of excellent customer service and could potentially put the bank at risk because the data, such as account balances, weren't in real-time. Although everyone patiently explained that was "just the way it was," I was so blinded by youthful confidence that I requested permission to raise the issue to the bank president. I thought carefully about the background and key points I needed to make in my pitch and practiced these points out loud for several days. The bank president listened to my story and agreed with my reasoning. By the next weekend, we had full computer access in the bank drive-thru. This incident solidified my realization that a good story can influence change.

After completing an internship with ASHP, I knew I wanted to embark on a nontraditional pharmacy path, applying the knowledge I had gained in pharmacy school in the field of health policy. I decided to apply for ASHP's Executive Residency in Association Management and Leadership, and I knew I needed a letter of intent that would set me apart from the other candidates. I brainstormed for several weeks and finally decided to write about how choosing the ASHP residency was similar to shopping for my green dining room table. In my letter, I shared that when shopping for a table, I immediately fell in love with a green dining room table at the first store I visited. But, I made myself visit almost every other furniture store in town just to make sure I had found the perfect one, especially since this constituted one of the first big purchases on my own and my mother didn't think it was the most practical long-term decision. Similarly, health policy felt like a perfect fit as soon as I stepped through those ASHP doors, merging my passions about the vital role of pharmacists in healthcare with leadership and problem-solving. Yet, I knew I needed to explore the multitude of possibilities that the pharmacy profession offered in my various experiential rotations before making a decision on my future—just like shopping for my green table. Using an analogy of table shopping to outline my interest in the ASHP residency was a bit of a risk, but that story created the impact I needed. In fact, long after my residency ended, selection committee staff would refer to my memorable "green table" essay, asking me to share the story with a colleague or a student. I'm also pleased to report that after more than 15 years, that green table still resides in my dining room.

I expanded on the art of storytelling to deliver results as the ASHP executive resident and later as an ASHP staff member. While preparing a presentation on avian influenza and emergency preparedness, I thought about what message would most resonate with the pharmacists in the audience and motivate them to modify their current practices. When I was coordinating ASHP's official position on a new FDA postmarketing surveillance policy, I collaborated with staff to compile a variety of facts and viewpoints from ASHP members into a cohesive and compelling explanation of our concerns. It was instrumental that we, as staff, connect those policy priorities to the critical work ASHP members were doing in developing ASHP's leadership agenda and professional policies. And, then, we would utilize those stories to advocate to Congress, other government agencies, professional associations, and the public about the invaluable role of pharmacists on the frontlines of healthcare.

Several years later, I began working for the FDA as Industry Liaison in the Office of External Affairs. I built or worked to strengthen relationships between the Agency and industry trade associations representing the broad range of FDA-regulated products, including human and veterinary drugs, medical devices, and the nation's food supply. To create these types of connections, it was paramount to understand the "story" of these groups—their priorities and how those priorities intersected with the ongoing initiatives and mission of FDA.

As I became involved in assessing the impact of major Agency announcements on the industry groups I oversaw, it became evident how critical our messaging, or the ability to clearly communicate why FDA took a certain action, was to the success of the announcement. FDA actions have tremendous, and often, global impacts on industry, health professionals, and consumers. How those stakeholders, including the media and Congress, comprehend the importance and the effect of those actions directly relate to the FDA's ability to explain the policy in a simple and straightforward manner. A poor message could cause confusion, even panic, and could yield negative consequences for the Agency. The story, and how it is delivered, truly matters.

Now in FDA's Office of Policy, a major component of my work focuses on helping the Agency develop solutions for a specific policy outcome, taking into account limitations stemming from scientific capabilities, regulations, or legislation. For example, to respond to continued interest from Congress, industry, and other stakeholders about FDA's regulatory oversight of combination medical products—products that include prefilled syringes or drug-eluting stents—it is imperative for the Agency to clearly articulate its current efforts and address any concerns raised. Crafting an effective narrative, or story, of how the solution works while taking into account these various constraints has proven as essential to a successful outcome as the analysis used to construct the solution.

When developing policy recommendations, I first formulate a framework by asking myself, or the group I'm leading, a few critical questions: What problem are we attempting to solve? What behaviors do we want to change? Who is our audience—those affected by the problem and those affected by the potential solution? What newspaper headline would we want to read to let us know that our policy solution had worked? By addressing these questions, we are able to conceptualize the desired outcome and work backwards on what policy options can achieve it. We tell the "future" story in order to make a plan for today.

Policy development, especially at a federal agency like FDA, can be a complicated and sometimes lengthy process with many stops, starts, and twists along the road as new evidence, new input from stakeholders, and new priorities emerge. The message often requires revision over time as issues arise and additional constraints must be considered. Regardless, this storytelling exercise is helpful in moving ideas forward and similar to a "vision board" one might develop as a part of any goal setting—whether personal or professional. Envisioning the story helps establish a map of sorts to measure against as the policy develops, creates a simple narrative that can be used when getting leadership or stakeholder buy-in, and serves to mobilize and motivate the group around its identified mission or desired outcome.

Storytelling is a powerful tool no matter what field of pharmacy you pursue. A personal story can instantly set a patient at ease or create camaraderie with a new colleague or team. You can maximize an educational opportunity—whether it's with a room full of health professionals or with a single patient—by considering not just the facts to be presented but also the best way to organize and present the information so it resonates with the audience in front of you. If you have to advocate to your senior leadership about the desire to start a new service or you need additional resources, it's advantageous to develop a clear narrative, including an illustration of how your request aligns with and helps them accomplish their priorities. When confronted with a difficult or complex problem, imagine the headline you would want someone to write; then, work backwards to identify alternatives that can make your envisioned solution a reality.

Finally, as a young pharmacist, one of the most important stories you need to develop is your own. Spend time talking with leaders in pharmacy and in other disciplines to hear and learn from their personal journeys. Tell others about your career goals so that they can be an advocate for you as future opportunities arise. Perhaps most importantly, define what professional success looks like for you in

30 years, and then work backwards to understand what steps you should take to achieve that goal.

Everyone loves a good story, so be intentional about making yours great.

All the best,

Lesley

Christina Y. Martin, PharmD, MS

Go Forth with an Open Mind and Be Passionate About What You Do

A self-described "Type A planner," Christina views her busy life as a constant motion involving the juggling of five balls: work, family, health, friends, and spirit. Being especially busy during her residency training, she came up with strategies to ensure that all of these important balls stayed in the air. As a millennial, it is no surprise that Christina's strategies involved the use of technology, including ASHP's Connect platform to network with her professional colleagues. An advanced pharmacy practice experience (APPE) rotation during her last year as a student pharmacist ignited her interest in association management as a career path and led to her current role at ASHP.

Christina Y. Martin is currently Director of Membership Forums at ASHP. Before joining the ASHP staff, Christina was Pharmacy Supervisor at Ann B. Barshinger Cancer Institute at Lancaster General Health in Lancaster, Pennsylvania. She received her PharmD degree at the University of Pittsburgh and a MS in Pharmacy Practice Management at the University of Kansas, where she also completed a combined postgraduate year (PGY) 1 and PGY2 residency in health-system pharmacy administration. She is an active member of the American Society of Association Executives, currently serving on the Young Professionals Committee. Outside of pharmacy, Christina practices Bikram yoga and enjoys home brewing with her husband.

Christina advises: **Go forth with an open mind, be passionate about what you do, and share your strategies about how to juggle those five balls.**

Dear Young Pharmacist,

Although my current responsibilities as an association executive no longer deem me an essential employee, it is still essential that I continue to juggle the balls of work, family, health, friends, and spirit. The transition from residency to workforce was especially difficult to manage, and I would have benefitted immensely from the career transition resources that are now available to students and residency graduates. I am excited that we are more transparent in our conversations and more honest about those transitions.

More than 4,000 residents are transitioning into the workforce each year. We jokingly call the first post-residency job a "PGY3" (postgraduate year 3) and spend weeks to months (the first 90 days) exploring how we start juggling those five balls again. One strategy that worked for me, as a Type A planner, was to schedule the activities corresponding to those five balls on my work calendar. Scheduling a 5:15 p.m. yoga class on my work calendar held me accountable to leaving the hospital by 4:50 p.m. I shouldn't neglect mentioning that there were exceptions to the rule—drug shortages that required immediate attention, picking up a staffing shift during peak flu season, and unscheduled disruptions to information system interfaces—but integrating family picnics or happy hours with friends into my calendar helped keep the juggling act in motion.

Similarly, I scheduled local chapter meetings and ASHP advisory group conference calls on my work calendar. Some employers perceive volunteer organizational involvement as part of the work day, while others view it as an extracurricular activity. It is important to clarify which stance your employer (or future employer) holds on organizational involvement. For me, I've worked for both, but I didn't let that deter my decisions to attend a state society meeting or skip lunch so that I could participate in a committee conference call. The intangible benefits of participating in a conference call, learning from my peers, and having an opportunity to ask a practice issue question to a seasoned practitioner overfilled my bucket more so than a 30-minute lunch break.

I am frequently asked if I miss direct patient care activities and if I will return to pharmacy practice. I'm still at a point where I've been in association management for fewer years than I practiced as a licensed pharmacist. My earliest pharmacy experiences were as a pharmacy technician in a chain grocery store pharmacy for 3 years before working and learning in a community teaching hospital. I thrived on the "every day presents new challenges" phenomenon as a pharmacy intern and immediately knew that hospital and health-system pharmacy was my desired end-point. I enjoyed taking ownership of operational responsibilities while fulfilling inpatient pharmacy technician responsibilities, as well as incorporating didactic training into clinically oriented projects with our inpatient pharmacists and clinical specialists.

In reflecting on the satisfaction and motivation that those earliest health-system experiences afforded me, it is not surprising that *responsibility* and *input* are my top two strengths (per the Clifton StrengthsFinder assessment). I enjoy all aspects of hospital pharmacy practice and never had the urge to be a clinical pharmacy specialist. I think back to the annual career fairs that were held in Salk Hall at the University of Pittsburgh School of Pharmacy where my classmates congregated around the tables for the career paths they were pursuing. I thought that if I had an opportunity to "see it all," then perhaps I could narrow the list and identify what type of expert I would become in the pharmacy profession.

When we were beginning to think about APPE rotations in the fall of P3 year, our Student Society of Health-System Pharmacy (SSHP) faculty advisor suggested that I pursue a rotation at ASHP headquarters for one of my elective rotation blocks. Our faculty advisor had completed a summer internship at ASHP headquarters while he was a student pharmacist, so he understood how impactful first-hand experiences are on one's career. I accepted his advice and applied for an APPE rotation in September of my P4 year. My advisor highly recommended the month of September so I would be on site during the ASHP policy week. Little did I know that this rotation experience at ASHP headquarters in Bethesda, Maryland, would be a milestone in my career decisions and a major influence in my personal choices.

Similar to any APPE rotation—acute care, community, and institutional—a significant portion of the rotation was dedicated to project work and professional development. One of the rotation's unique aspects was being encouraged to set up meetings with the senior leadership team, including Dr. Henri Manasse who was the Chief Executive Officer at that time. It was during those one-on-one meetings where I learned about these ASHP leaders' career paths and how they eventually ended up on staff at the organization's headquarters. There was not a "one-size-fits-all" model and with backgrounds in academia, home infusion, informatics, and medication safety, most never expected to work for a professional association. They held past roles such as staff pharmacist, clinical coordinator, director of pharmacy, and professor. A handful had completed residency training in pharmacy administration, which opened the door to diverse opportunities within the profession. These one-on-one meetings at ASHP headquarters solidified my decision to pursue residency training in health-system pharmacy administration.

During one of the residency interviews, I was asked about my post-residency and 5-year career goals. Now remember, I had only just decided to pursue a health-system pharmacy administration residency 5 months prior because of the diverse opportunities that administration alumni had pursued post-residency. How was I to know how 2 years of residency training might influence my future decisions? In hindsight, and also now from my experiences with precepting students and residents, it was okay to *not* have all the answers about the future. Students and residents with a narrow focus have been highly successful in attaining their career goals. However, I also witnessed some who have been disappointed when life gave them a bump; in those situations, they didn't know how to react. The successful students and residents were those who had a plan but were adaptable to change and willing to make adjustments along the way.

Residency has been, by far, one of the hardest times in my life but also one of the most rewarding experiences. Involvement with professional associations during residency allowed me to juggle the balls of work, family, health, friends, and spirit. Let me explain how. Using ASHP's listserve, now ASHP Connect, I was able to query my pharmacy colleagues across the country as I **work**ed on research projects. Our calls with the New Practitioners Forum Advisory Group often allotted 5-10 minutes at the end to discuss issues we were encountering or to share strategies for success. Colleagues with whom I collaborated on advisory group deliverables have become personal **friends**—we now vacation together and attend one another's weddings and baby showers.

Using ASHP resources to augment my practice area allowed me to be an active participant on my rotations and through my multidisciplinary committee work. It was refreshing to see how pieces of a professional organization (e.g., journal articles, publications, on-demand webinars, professional meetings) made my daily work easier, which resulted in an increased **spirit**. Attending ASHP meetings always helped me recharge my energy for the profession as well as gather innovative ideas to take back to my workplace.

Wanting to absorb as much information as possible during my residency, I made sure to maintain my **health** so that I didn't miss a day of rotation and promoted healthy behaviors to my rounding team and my patients. Finally, my **family** constantly said how proud they were, which inspired me to continue nurturing my personal and professional growth. In residency, I cared for patients during evening, weekend, and holiday staffing shifts that covered the internal medicine and solid organ transplant services. As a supervisor, I cared for my staffs of pharmacists and technicians who were caring for patients. As an association executive, I now care for members who are caregivers for other pharmacy staff, non-pharmacy staff, and patients.

I mentioned earlier that the rotation experience at ASHP headquarters was not only a milestone for career decisions but also a major influence for personal choices. My rotation dates overlapped by 1 week with a student pharmacist from The Medical University of South Carolina College of Pharmacy and a student pharmacist from McWhorter School of Pharmacy at Samford University. These two individuals who I met at 7272 Wisconsin Avenue (ASHP headquarters location in 2009) started as professional acquaintances and are now close, personal friends. We catch up at the ASHP Midyear Clinical Meeting and Summer Meetings, have visited each other in our home states, and have become friends with each other's spouses. It was our desire to learn that acquainted us as P4 students, but our desire to advance the profession and practice has strengthened that bond through the years.

I will end my letter with this final story. Just recently, my mother commented that she knew I would end up working for ASHP. You know how mothers are— sometimes they will say anything in the best interest of their children, so I semi-laughed off her comment. She replied and said, "No, really. You came home from that rotation and were so excited about the pharmacy profession. I remember you said, 'Mom, that would be a cool place to work someday.' And knowing you [Christina], when you put your mind to it, you are disciplined to do it." Mothers know best.

Go forth with an open mind, be passionate about what you do, and share your strategies about how to juggle those five balls of work, family, health, friends, and spirit.

Best regards,

Christina

Katherine (Kat) A. Miller, PharmD, MHA

Network and Think About What Makes a Good Boss

Kat outlines from her personal experience five key characteristics of good bosses: they listen, ask you how you want to tackle a project before telling you how to do it, expose you to growth opportunities, may let you fail but not let you fall, and keep in touch. Based on her recent experience, she discusses how to approach the decision to change positions.

Katherine (Kat) A. Miller is currently Director, System Inpatient Clinical Services, University of Kansas Health System. Previously she was Assistant Director, Pharmacy Operations, the University of Chicago Medicine. Kat received her PharmD from the University of Wisconsin and her MHA from Simmons College. She completed a postgraduate year (PGY) 1 pharmacy practice residency and a PGY2 health system pharmacy administration specialty residency at the Oregon Health and Sciences University.

Kat's advice is: **Network at meetings and conferences so that when jobs are available, your name comes up in the conversation. Consider the characteristics of a good boss and how that will impact your career decisions.**

Dear Young Pharmacist,

As you continue to grow through your career, one of your toughest decisions will be leaving one position for another. You may decide that you need to move across the country for career or personal reasons, to work with a different boss or team, to have more opportunities and career growth, or to decrease your responsibilities and focus on other areas of your life. All of these, and other reasons, are valid. If you are continuing to meet expectations in your position, no one but you can decide when it is time to look for a new opportunity.

Let me tell you about how I made that decision the first time. I was about 3½ years into my first position out of residency and was lucky to be hired into a team that worked very well together, allowed me to develop my leadership style with mentoring from my Director, and exposed me to other leaders in pharmacy across the city and state. I was happy, I was learning, and I wasn't sure I was looking for a change.

During my time in that role, my Director exposed me to new experiences and mentored me in preparation for my next position, although I knew she didn't want me to leave. She encouraged me to be involved at the system and hospital level for informatics and operations. I was surprised to find that one of my least exhilarating rotations during residency turned out to be an extremely good fit for me, and informatics has been an area of growth and interest of mine ever since. I was asked to lead projects, which exposed me to nursing and physician colleagues. I was also given opportunities to be involved in state and local organizations, which enhanced my networking, project management, and leadership opportunities and skills. If you are lucky enough to work for someone who is able and willing to provide you with these learning opportunities—take them! Don't forget to ask for feedback along the way. As painful as it is, you are more likely to learn from your failures and missteps than from your successes (although those are fun, too).

Big projects were on the horizon—things I was excited to participate in at my hospital. However, something was missing. I was at a point where I was ready for more responsibility but wasn't ready to be a director. I have to admit, when I was in your shoes, I didn't think I'd ever be ready or interested in being a director. However, as I gained more experience, I decided it was something I would definitely consider. That being said, I wasn't really sure how to go about looking for my next position. But as it turned out, I didn't have to.

This is where all that networking you do at meetings and conferences comes in handy. When jobs open up, your name may be mentioned in conversation. You may have a former colleague, employer, or employee recommend you. I was lucky enough to be in this situation when I received a call about a job similar to mine but in an academic medical center. I had completed my residency in an academic medical center. Although I truly enjoyed my experiences at a community hospital in a large health system, the breadth of experiences at an academic medical center was appealing to me.

It was a hard decision, but I knew that moving into this new role would open more doors for me in the future. More opportunities were available for transitioning into various roles within this same institution. As a result, in my 2 years at that academic medical center, I held three different roles. I gained valuable experiences and learned from new leaders and colleagues. None of this would have been possible had I stayed in my first position. There are things I haven't experienced today that I would potentially be able to do had I not transitioned, but the same is true because I did.

A mentor once told me, "If you're comfortable, you're not learning." This phrase has stuck with me. I can't say that I was "comfortable" in my role, but I was ready to accept that a change was in order. Whether you are searching out a change or someone is asking you to change, I have a few recommendations:

- **Find someone you can talk to who understands your professional goals.** This may be your current supervisor, or it may be a former colleague or mentor. Find someone you can trust who will put your interests first. Be open and honest with him or her and ask them to do the same.

- **Decide who you want to ask to be a reference.** Avoid situations where you are asked to provide references when you haven't already secured positive responses from those individuals you have identified. Be proactive and ask two to four people if they can provide a strong, positive reference. Identify people from different points in your career who can speak to your various strengths and weaknesses with solid examples.

- **Tell your boss.** This is a hard one but if you have a positive, professional relationship with your boss, it is important for him or her to know you are considering a different position. You may want to ask your boss to be a reference. That person may want to know if you can be convinced to stay in your position by being offered additional opportunities and professional development.

- **Find someone outside of the pharmacy profession to talk to.** For me, this is my parents. I always talk to them when I am considering big career changes and opportunities. They think about my options and choices in a different way than I do, ask questions, provide guidance (sometimes whether I want it or not), and always trust and support my decisions.

As I moved through my residency training and first years in leadership and talked with colleagues in similar roles, we discussed what we like and don't like about our roles. Being able to "own" projects, make our own decisions, and be supported rank high on our lists. I know you have heard that the #1 reason people leave their jobs is because of their bosses. Although this was not the reason I made my transition, it is important to consider who your boss will be when you are considering a new position.

The following are key characteristics of good bosses:

- **They listen.** They actually listen. They lock their computer screen, close the door, face you, and LISTEN! They listen to really understand what you are saying. And if they're a great boss, they understand when you need advice versus when you just need to vent.

- **They ask you how you want to tackle a project before telling you how to do it.** They throw out guard rails and say come back if you need help. They guide you to finding your own solution rather than directing the solution.

- **They expose you to growth opportunities.** It may mean they opt out of a high visibility project to give you the learning opportunity, or it may mean they recommend you for additional committees and groups. This may not always be easy or comfortable, but they know it will enhance your growth.

- **They may let you fail, but they won't let you fall.** They definitely won't let you fall on your face in public, and they will help you understand how to do things differently next time. They may also take responsibility for failure or direct it toward a larger team effort than single you out to ensure you continue growing in your role.

- **They keep in touch.** They honestly want to know that you're continuing to be successful in your next role. If you are both lucky, you may work together again in the future.

After you make the decision to move to a new role, consider your transition plan. We have all witnessed our colleagues' successful and unsuccessful transitions. I recommend you document your projects and then identify next steps and the key stakeholders who can tackle the work. Prioritize your projects. Leave detailed notes on your direct reports so the person who follows you can be successful, too. Most importantly, don't burn any bridges.

You have experienced transition previously. You graduated from pharmacy school and possibly moved across the country for your residency. You learned everything you could during your residency and received a fabulous offer for your first position. You are learning how to be a new leader, and you are having fun. Transitions are a part of life. Sometimes they happen when we least expect them— enjoy them and don't be afraid.

I wish you all the best in your future pharmacy endeavors, as I know you will celebrate successes.

Warmly,

Kat

Kathleen (Kathy) S. Pawlicki, MS, FASHP

It's Not Easy, But a Gal Can Have It All—Family and Successful Career

Kathy traces her career and personal life evolution, offering specifics that can benefit others, while sharing how she jointly raises children with her husband. She explains that intertwining career and family are just part of normal day-to-day living. There are times when work requires more attention and other times when family requires more—the key is to know when one requires more attention over the other.

Kathleen (Kathy) S. Pawlicki is currently Vice President and Chief Pharmacist at Beaumont Health with responsibility for pharmacy at one of the largest health systems in Michigan. Previously she was Administrative Director, Professional Services at Beaumont Hospital, with responsibilities for pharmacy and also several non-pharmacy departments. Kathy has served on the ASHP Board of Directors and as Chair of the ASHP Section of Pharmacy Practice Managers. She received her undergraduate degree in Pharmacy from Ferris State and her MS from Wayne State College of Pharmacy. Kathy completed a pharmacy residency at Providence Hospital, Southfield, Michigan.

Kathy's advice: **Take the first step and get involved in your career beyond your "day job," and do something every year to recommit to that involvement.**

Dear Young Pharmacist,

When I graduated from high school, I had no expectations for what life would have in store for me. My only hopes were to graduate from college, get a good job, have a family, and contribute to the world in a meaningful way. Growing up in a small, rural farming town in the middle of Michigan, I would never have imagined the career opportunities and possibilities I have had the privilege to experience. Working hard, taking advantage of opportunities, and committing to family and community were fundamental to my parents' belief system in their actions and words. Little did I know that these foundational principles would provide the tools and beliefs necessary to be successful in pursuing a career in pharmacy. Of course, it was up to *me* to put those qualities into action.

I always knew I would go to college, but I didn't have a clear career path. Only after I stumbled into a pharmacy one day to buy a medication did I consider pharmacy as a career. I met my husband (also a pharmacy student) while in pharmacy school, and we were married 2 weeks after graduation. When I entered the workforce in the early 1980s, I quickly began chiseling a career for myself as I learned about residencies and hospital pharmacy management tracks. I wondered how I could juggle a career and have a family at the same time. In my first years of practice, I asked several women for the key to successfully accomplishing this. I quickly learned that no one had the answer.

One would think that 30 years later, somewhere along the way, the question would be answered. However, I still see young men and women struggling with the same question and finding no perfect solution. What I have found as key ingredients are the same values my parents instilled in me: hard work, leverage opportunities, and commitment.

My husband and I have raised three children who are all successful in their own careers (a lawyer, an engineer, and a college sophomore—hopeful accountant). Managing both home and work life required hard work and a lot of organization, but it was all worth it in the end. For me, that meant late nights after the kids were in bed answering emails and working on projects, sharing the responsibilities at home with my spouse, and going the extra mile with my children. I was bound and determined that a two-income household would not prohibit my children from getting involved in activities. For us, this meant organizing our schedules to accommodate family. My husband took morning duty of breakfast and seeing them off to school; I took evenings, filled with pick-ups from daycare or driving them to activities.

I fulfilled my desire to become involved in professional organizations in those early years by sticking to local associations that required limited travel. I also felt it was important for my kids to have an understanding of where I went every day, rather than leave it to their imagination of why mom disappeared early in the mornings and was up late doing work. To satisfy my mind (and I hope my kids' curiosity), I made sure they visited my work occasionally and especially when I changed jobs. And finally, I made a personal commitment to myself that my children would have a home-cooked meal every night. So, we created a routine of shopping and cooking the following week's meals every Sunday. (I must confess we might have relied a little too heavily on crockpot meals, based on the looks I get from them now when I mention a good crockpot recipe!)

I sometimes chuckle at "work-life balance" comments. For me, work is career and career is part of my life. Hence, intertwining career and family are the norm and just part of living. Sometimes work requires more attention and sometimes family requires more—it is all relative to the moment and making sure you know when one requires more attention over the other.

In the early years of my career, I started doing one thing right without even realizing it. When talking with other pharmacy managers and leaders, I listened carefully to what they were doing and the opportunities they took advantage of to advance their careers. Initially, this listening and learning resulted in my obtaining a hospital pharmacy residency and a Master's degree in Hospital Pharmacy Administration.

Through each career experience, I learned another important lesson. If you focus on your current responsibilities by working hard and doing what is right for patients/staff/organization, new opportunities will arise. This has proven true throughout my career. My focus on changing pharmacy practice to support hospital goals resulted in a chance to lead a hospital process improvement initiative focused on multiple areas of operations throughout the institution. This door opened another to have administrative responsibility for several other departments. I find that each increase in responsibility requires more work, chances to practice what I have learned, and experiences to learn new skills. Today, I am fortunate to say that I have been a Director of Pharmacy at three facilities, a Hospital Administrator responsible for several non-pharmacy departments, and now Vice President and Chief Pharmacist. I know my learning is not complete, but the challenge of contributing to the work and care of others continues to motivate and inspire me.

Just as my father was a businessman committed to the small community we lived in, pharmacy is my community that I dedicate my loyalty to. In a small high school, in a small town, getting involved is pretty easy. If you talk to your classmates and listen to your teachers, you can learn about volunteer opportunities to make contributions to your school and classmates. Professional organizations work much the same way. After my residency, during my first job, the Director of Pharmacy asked if I was interested in being a newsletter Co-Editor for the regional health-system pharmacy organization. This single step to become involved in creating a successful newsletter opened up opportunities to become Banquet Chair followed by Secretary, Treasurer, and ultimately President for the organization. What I didn't realize at the time was that local involvement overlaps with state involvement. Hence, as President of the local association in Michigan, you are a Board representative to the state organization, and this begets opportunities to be involved at the state level, which in turn is a great introduction to involvement at the national level. For me, it resulted in becoming a Delegate for Michigan in the ASHP House of Delegates. I cannot emphasize enough the true value of involvement in local and state organizations and the importance of networking and connecting with others in the profession.

Through work at local and state level organizations, I was asked to become Program Chair for the ASHP Section of Pharmacy Practice Managers. Introduction to section activities through this role eventually lead to section Chair. At the conclusion of my section leadership responsibilities, ASHP embarked on a Task Force for Organizational Affairs. Having had state affiliate leadership experience and recent ASHP experience in the section (and the House of Delegates), I was asked to serve. The task force's focus was to evaluate the current membership structure and policy development process for the society. As in the past, I couldn't say "no" to this opportunity to do more work for my community. During the involvement with the task force, I was fortunate to also be elected as a Board member to the ASHP Board of Directors. Although I have just completed my term as a Board member and I don't know what my next opportunity to the profession will be, I am confident something is right around the corner that requires a "yes" response.

Each new role and responsibility is an opportunity to contribute to the work of others in your community, providing new experiences to practice old skills and learn new ones. Each opportunity has the possibility of leading to the next opportunity. I wouldn't change anything in my career path—each step along the way was important to my development and understanding of patient care and professional organizations.

Although the work is hard, the rewards are great. My advice to new practitioners is: (1) take the first step and get involved in your career beyond your "day job," and (2) do something every year to recommit to that involvement.

And don't forget what I learned along the way:

- Be loyal and committed to your community and family.
- Work hard.
- Take advantage of opportunities (say YES).

Good luck with your future, and never underestimate what you can accomplish.

Kathy

Nirali Rana, PharmD

Leadership Roles Allow You to Be Present at Work and at Life

If you want to learn how to oversee 70 community pharmacies, conduct and precept community pharmacy residency programs, and remain active in professional organization leadership while raising children, then you will enjoy this letter. Nirali encourages you to be active in the political process and join non-pharmacy healthcare organizations as well as pharmacy organizations because there is strength in numbers for achieving the end goal—continuous improvement of patient care.

Nirali Rana is currently Area Healthcare Supervisor, Boston, Walgreen Company. Previously, she was District Pharmacy Manager for Walgreen. She received her PharmD degree from Northeastern University.

Nirali's advice is: *Effective delegation is the key to success. Involvement in organizations including ASHP, APhA, and internal business resource groups will help you to recognize the obstacles that we all face and find ways to overcome them.*

Dear Young Pharmacist,

"Far and away the best prize that life offers is the chance to work hard at work worth doing." —Theodore Roosevelt

One of the best decisions I made in my life was to attend Northeastern University School of Pharmacy. Being a pharmacist is extremely rewarding and impactful. Those who are able to do what they love every day are incredibly blessed. Throughout pharmacy school I experienced several facets of the pharmacy field, but community pharmacy always felt like home to me. It's where I developed relationships with my patients, where I truly felt and saw my impact, and where I found my family at work. I have a HUGE family both professionally and personally.

As you grow into your professional careers, make sure you network and develop relationships with people who can be your advocate, teacher, and friend. Along the way, you will also have coaches, mentors, and sponsors. You may be thinking: What's the difference between a coach, mentor, and sponsor? The simple answer is this: a coach talks *to* you, a mentor talks *with* you, and a sponsor talks *about* you. Make sure to take full advantage of these relationships. As my career has developed, I've been able to fulfill all of these roles.

If you LOVE people, people LOVE you, and you LOVE working in a community pharmacy, then you owe it to the profession to work in a community pharmacy. I thoroughly enjoyed managing several pharmacies, but I felt a need to grow into an expanded leadership role so I could have a greater impact and influence change. Our community pharmacists need to be supported in a manner that positions them to provide excellent patient care. It's not an easy job and deserves more credit than it receives. If you're doing it just for the money, you'll never be happy. It's not fair for you, your patients, or the employees that work alongside you.

Community pharmacists are the most accessible healthcare providers; however, pharmacists are not recognized as such. This baffles me. According to IMS Health data, the United States incurs $300 billion in healthcare expenditures due to medication adherence issues. We continually see studies of pharmacists having an impact on patient care and decreasing healthcare expenditures. I envision a world in community pharmacy where our time with patients is valued. Patients should have the opportunity to see pharmacists, and pharmacists should have the opportunity to see patients. My hope is that by the time you read this letter, we have made the first steps in enacting federal legislation to include pharmacists as healthcare providers. The next steps will be in changing the infrastructure of healthcare to streamline the inclusion of pharmacists as an integral part of the healthcare team.

It is essential we use our skills, training, and experience to benefit patients. My goal is to help you achieve this through my letter. As difficult as it may be, the importance of providing medication therapy management and immunizations on a consistent basis is crucial to demonstrate the impact of our profession. Our daily priorities can easily push these activities aside, but we need to find a way to educate our patients and work together to better advocate for those patients, our profession, and ourselves.

I would highly recommend strengthening your skills in people leadership on a continual basis and increasing your EIQ (emotional intelligence quotient). There are many books and articles on this topic. Sign up for daily or weekly emails from Fastcompany.com, *Harvard Business Review*, Mindtools.com, Gallup.com, and HRDQ.com. These tools, along with your supervisors and human resources personnel, will supply the skills you need to lead a high-performing team. Using effective process improvement strategies such as Lean Six Sigma and following standard operating procedures will enable you and your team to have more time to treat your patients and properly determine their healthcare needs.

What else can we do to change the healthcare landscape? Join professional organizations, especially the state associations. There is strength in numbers. The American Medical Association has been successful in changing legislation due to their impact from their number of members. Also, contact legislators in your district to educate them on the bills that will positively impact your profession. Since my introduction to the Massachusetts Pharmacist Association (MPhA), American Pharmacists Association (APhA), and ASHP, I have had an entirely new mindset as far as how I can champion change in our profession. The more I learned, the more the fire grew inside me. I had to be a part of these amazing organizations working to improve the way we view healthcare. Last year I was voted into a Governor-at-Large position for MPhA and have enjoyed every moment. I organized an event at the State House for American Pharmacists Month where we educated 40 legislators about the state pharmacist provider status bill. I was extremely proud of what we were able to accomplish over a couple of months. Your active participation in the state professional associations makes a huge difference—the associations are only as good as their members. My involvement in ASHP, MPhA, and APhA has resulted in my becoming a stronger advocate, pharmacist, and leader. Each one of us as individuals makes a difference.

I rely on many of the resources listed above. But one competency I always try to improve is optimizing efficiency and productivity in my work while still having the same amount of energy for my family when I get home. I have 4-year-old boy/girl twins and a 6-year-old son as well as an incredibly supportive husband, Rohit, of 12 years. I never want to wish I had spent more time with my family. Instead, I put everything into the hours at work, and then I put everything into the time at home . . . at least I try to. I have not always had this skill of balance. When I was on leave after my twins were born, I was promoted from managing one pharmacy to overseeing 35 pharmacies. That was far from an easy transition. In fact, it was extremely difficult. It took me many months to realize that I did not have balance. My time and energy was spent mostly on the work side of my life instead of the family side. I soon realized this was not what I wanted. I had to figure out how to better manage my time. By listening to the advice from my peers, supervisors, friends, and family, I was able to reprioritize and rebalance my work-life scale. One piece of valuable advice reminded me there's always work to do, so I would have to emphatically state "Ok, I did what I could today; now it's time for me and my family." If you need improvement in your time management skills, I would recommend downloading the "Top Three to Do List" app. It helps me ensure I finish my major tasks each day.

I know many women leaders deal with these work-life balance issues all the time. This is a perfect segue into a popular topic in business—women in leadership. Women are making up a larger percentage of each graduating pharmacy class. However, we see fewer women in the leadership roles of greater responsibility. Many women do not believe they will be able to balance leadership and life, so they do not pursue leadership positions. If balance is what's stopping you, then you should look at me as an example. I strive every day to become a better role model and maintain balance between my leadership responsibilities and my roles as wife and mother.

With support from your family, friends, and colleagues, it is possible to enjoy the best of both worlds. A leadership role actually provides flexibility to be present both at work and home. You just have to be honest with yourself, your partner, and co-workers. Remember, you don't always have to say "yes" to every project or do everything yourself. You don't always have to be 100% ready for that next role—no one is ever 100% ready. Doing everything yourself doesn't give others the opportunity to develop. Effective delegation is the key to success. Again, my involvement in organizations like ASHP, APhA, and internal business resource groups such as Women of Walgreens has helped me to recognize the obstacles that we all face and find ways to overcome them.

In my current role as an Area Healthcare Supervisor, I oversee 70 pharmacies. I influence approximately 240 pharmacists without direct supervision. This is possible because I have developed relationships with these pharmacists and the managers leading them. I have walked in their shoes, and they know that what I say comes from a genuine place. I care about them as employees and as unique individuals. I have always had an innate way of connecting with people, but I truly believe the energy I put into becoming a better leader has also helped me. I recommend you do the same—there's always room for improvement.

Currently, Walgreens has 20 community pharmacy residency programs with 22 resident positions available across the nation. We have four programs in Massachusetts, where I have been fortunate to be a preceptor. I am able to pay it forward by providing the leadership development component of the program. These residency programs have helped set these pharmacists apart from other community pharmacists. They are exposed to top leadership in the region, learn innovative ways to expand the profession, and obtain a teaching certificate. We view the residency programs as a training ground for our specialty locations, but it's also a way for our most talented pharmacists to be set on a fast track to leadership. Each year, we work to improve these programs so that our residents receive the experience they need to get a competitive edge.

I am truly honored to share my experiences and advice with you. As you grow in your career and turn into rising stars yourselves, please remember to get involved in pharmacy organizations as well as organizations outside of pharmacy in the public health/population health arena. We all need to do a better job connecting with important stakeholders. Pharmacists are not well represented in healthcare professional organizations. I recently joined the Massachusetts Health Council and hope to educate some members of that community.

I have confidence our profession will be recognized for what we truly are—healthcare providers. I am excited to see our next generation of pharmacists take it to the next level. Thank you for everything you are doing and are going to do!

Sincerely,

Nirali

Carly Rodriguez, PharmD

Sometimes It's Not About What You Know, It's About Who You Know and What They Think About You

Carly admits that being in the right place at the right time has contributed to her success. It was her interest in volunteering in associations while she was a student pharmacist that led Carly to explore career opportunities in managed care pharmacy. She knew that a postgraduate year (PGY) 1 residency was likely the minimum prerequisite for landing an entry-level job in managed care, so she applied for the match. While applying for a residency, she stumbled upon—and landed—an attractive opportunity that would become her first managed care pharmacy role. Being in the right place at the right time can only get you so far, though, so Carly shares other tips for success, including building her professional network and taking every opportunity to give back to those who follow her.

Carly Rodriguez is currently Pharmacy Director of Clinical Innovation at Moda Health in Portland, Oregon. Before joining Moda Health, she was Manager of Clinical Pharmacy Services and Residency Program Director at OmedaRx. She received her PharmD degree at the University of Washington School of Pharmacy. Being true to her credo of giving back, Carly is an active member and volunteer in the Academy of Managed Care Pharmacy (AMCP), both at the national and local level, and is also a volunteer and guest lecturer at her alma mater.

Carly's advice is: **Remember that pharmacy is a small world, so you're always making an impression, whether good or bad, on other pharmacists who you may encounter in the future.**

Dear Young Pharmacist,

Depending on the region of the country you live in or what school of pharmacy you attended, you may have entered pharmacy school with a preconceived notion of what kind of pharmacist you're going (or not going) to be. I encourage you to keep an open mind because, the truth is, when I entered pharmacy school

I didn't even know it was possible to be a pharmacy director at a health plan or health insurance company, or what some might call a "managed care pharmacist."

So, how did I discover this path in pharmacy? It was through *curiosity, commitment,* and *volunteerism.* What I knew about myself going into pharmacy school was that I am analytical, love to problem-solve, enjoy research, and want to develop as a leader within the profession. I sought out opportunities within school (e.g., courses, projects, independent study) and outside of school (e.g., internships, volunteer opportunities) to pursue those interests and skills. In doing so, I discovered the AMCP. This organization opened my eyes to the potential of bettering the lives of hundreds, thousands, or even millions of patients at a time rather than patient-by-patient in a traditional pharmacy setting.

I discovered that pharmacists who work in the managed care arena get to evaluate newly approved medications, analyze trends in medication use and cost, and develop innovative programs to ensure clinically appropriate, safe, and cost-effective use of medications by large populations of people. So, I committed myself to learning as much as I possibly could about this pharmacy field by attending AMCP conferences and volunteering to moderate continuing education sessions. I signed up to participate in AMCP's rigorous annual competition aimed at evaluating a new medication (the Pharmacy & Therapeutics [P&T] Competition), completed an internship at a health plan, took elective courses in areas such as managed care and pharmacoeconomics, and signed up for advance pharmacy practice experiences (APPEs) related to managed care.

My managed care internship, coursework, and APPE rotations solidified that this was the right career path for me. As I approached graduation from my PharmD program, I applied to managed care ASHP-accredited residency programs. Through this application process, I became aware of a pharmacist position available at the site where I had completed my internship. I found myself in the exact right place at the exact right time and was fortunate to enter the managed care field as a pharmacist without a residency. Let me emphasize the *exact right place at the exact right time* portion of my previous statement because the more common path to becoming a managed care pharmacist straight from pharmacy school is through residency training, which I am a huge proponent of! Residency training allows you to learn from seasoned pharmacists, gain exposure to aspects of pharmacy that you otherwise would not be exposed to as a staff pharmacist, complete a longitudinal project and seek publication, and develop leadership skills.

My first job in the field of managed care pharmacy was as a clinical pharmacist evaluating newly approved medications to determine how to best manage their use within a large health plan population. In this role, I was able to develop a management strategy for hepatitis C medications that encouraged clinically sound and cost-effective use. I also had numerous opportunities to interact with and present to other pharmacists and healthcare professionals including pharmacy technicians, nurses, and physicians. Additionally, I gained leadership skills through serving as an internship and APPE preceptor, the Residency Program Coordinator, and eventually the Residency Program Director.

The management skills that I gained through my company's APPE and residency opportunities gave me the necessary experience to pursue a manager position, which in turn allowed me to pursue a director-level position later in my career. Although I have achieved a level of management that I am satisfied with, I strive to continually build on my leadership skills. An important lesson that one of my mentors taught me is to recognize the difference between being a manager/director and being a leader. By definition, managers and directors manage and direct others within an organization. Employees who report to those positions follow their lead through a reporting structure but may or may not be aligned with their values or philosophies. On the other hand, leaders are those who others want to follow and choose to align with and support. Not all leaders are in management positions, and not everyone in a management position is a leader. My hope is that young pharmacists who want to develop into leaders and/or managers recognize the difference, and also realize that both distinctions are earned through hard work, commitment, and volunteerism over a sustained period of time.

Students and residents often ask me the best thing about being a managed care pharmacist, and I say there are so many great answers to this question. The one thing that stands out most is the ability to do something different every day. Each day, there are exciting new opportunities—a new drug gets approved, new evidence or guidelines are published related to a medication, a medication gets a new safety warning, or the price of a drug significantly increases. As a result, managed care pharmacists utilize different skills, gain new skills and knowledge, and interact with different types of professionals on a daily basis. Another great aspect of this pharmacy career path for me, as a pharmacist with a family, is that many managed care organizations operate during normal business hours and offer flexibility in terms of work schedules and locations.

Hopefully it is clear from my letter what the profession of managed care pharmacy has done for my career. But, how have I made a positive impact on managed care pharmacy? I'd like to think that it is through the same traits that brought me to this field in the first place—*curiosity, commitment,* and *volunteerism.* Curiosity led me, along with some other extremely dedicated managed care professionals, to ask "How can we increase the engagement in and awareness of managed care pharmacy issues in the Northwest?" By asking this question, doing some research, and collaborating with the national AMCP organization, we started the Northwest

Affiliate of AMCP with the goal of bringing managed care educational programming to our backyard.

The most rewarding contribution I've made to managed care pharmacy thus far is committing myself to further the profession by supporting the up-and-coming generation of managed care pharmacists. Whether guest lecturing in managed care electives, judging the P&T Competition, taking a few students to coffee or lunch, speaking in student sessions at national conferences, or promoting residency training, I am passionate about educating students on the impact one can make as a managed care pharmacist and the numerous paths to get there.

Lastly, volunteering is extremely important to me. National pharmacy organizations depend on volunteers to move initiatives and objectives forward and make pharmacy conferences a success. Each year of my career, I have served as an AMCP Committee member or chair, participated in advisory forums, and volunteered at national meetings in various roles. I fully embrace the philosophy that if I want to continue having a rewarding career, I must do my part to make the profession great.

I'd like to close by sharing some lessons, philosophies, and words of wisdom that I've learned throughout my career:

- **Get involved.** Join pharmacy organizations relevant to your field of pharmacy, volunteer to serve on committees or at conferences, or run for a Board position. This is a great way to stay up-to-date on the latest issues impacting your profession and also build your network.

- **Pharmacy is a small world.** You've likely heard this at least a hundred times, but I can't emphasize it enough. Remember that while on experiential rotations, at a job, or at a pharmacy conference, you're always making an impression—whether good or bad—on other pharmacists you may encounter in the future. The words of wisdom that have really stuck with me throughout my career are, "Sometimes it's not about what you know, it's about who you know and what they think about you."

- **Do your part to further the profession.** The legacy that you leave behind within your field of pharmacy can only be as strong as that field of pharmacy itself. Embrace opportunities to precept students, guest lecture, present in student sessions at pharmacy conferences, or serve as a diplomat or liaison between a national pharmacy organization and a school of pharmacy. Offer to call a student to talk about your pharmacy experience, your job, and your path to get there because a 30-minute phone call may be invaluable in shaping who that student might become as a pharmacist.

Sincerely,

Carly

Leigh Ann Ross, PharmD, BCPS, FASHP, FCCP

Work Hard, Seize Opportunities, and Dream Big

Leigh Ann was drawn to the profession of pharmacy at a young age, working alongside her pharmacist father in a community pharmacy. She assumed she would follow in his path, but fate stepped in during her residency training to steer her down a different path—academia and clinical practice. Once established in her career, Leigh Ann realized she could broaden her impact on the pharmacy profession and on healthcare through volunteer service. She was elected President of her state pharmacists' association, which offered her exposure to the health policy arena and ultimately to serve as a Health Policy Fellow for U.S. Senator Thad Cochran.

Leigh Ann Ross is Associate Dean for Clinical Affairs at the University of Mississippi School of Pharmacy, Professor in the Department of Pharmacy Practice, and Research Professor in the Research Institute of Pharmaceutical Sciences. She received her Bachelor's degree in Business Administration and her PharmD from the University of Mississippi and completed a primary care pharmacy residency at the University of Mississippi Medical Center. Leigh Ann is a former President of both the Mississippi Pharmacists Association and the Mississippi Biotechnology Association and a member of the American College of Clinical Pharmacy (ACCP) Board of Regents. She is an invited member of the National Academies of Practice and Pharmacy Academy as well as a Fellow of ACCP and ASHP.

Leigh Ann's advice is: **Work hard, seize opportunities, and dream big.**

Dear Young Pharmacist,

It seems like yesterday I was in your shoes filled with excitement to embark on a new career, yet somewhat nervous about the future. I encourage you to be excited. As a pharmacy educator, I fully appreciate your dedication and the hard work necessary to complete your degree and training. You should be proud, celebrate your accomplishments, and look forward to many more achievements in your career. Work hard, seize opportunities, and dream big!

The highlights I share from my career in pharmacy are shaped by my childhood experiences. I am fortunate for many reasons to be the daughter of Louis H. Ramsey, a retired pharmacist. He, along with his business partner Larry Young, owned Ramsey-Young Pharmacy in Pontotoc, Mississippi. I spent many days working in that pharmacy—dusting shelves, arranging the medications, and later helping fill prescriptions and talking with patients while in pharmacy school. I learned many important lessons in that independent pharmacy about our profession and about life. It was evident from watching my dad that he believed each person who walked through the door deserved respect. He, like many of his era, believed in hard work; he demonstrated this belief every day. I watched his impact on people—caring about them, meeting their needs in any way that he could, and cheering them up with a kind word or his sense of humor. I also observed a commitment to service in his community and our profession. Having my dad as an early role model, and the familiarity and relationships I developed growing up in the family business, steered my later decision for a career in pharmacy.

I focused my time as a student on successfully completing the pharmacy program at the University of Mississippi (UM) and believed I would practice in a setting much like my father. As I learned more about the future of pharmacy and other potential career opportunities, I saw value in completing a pharmacy residency program. I came to love the ambulatory care setting, where I had the opportunity to work as part of an interprofessional team of healthcare providers while maintaining that one-on-one, regular contact with patients I enjoyed from the community environment. I joined the faculty at my alma mater and began to teach pharmacy students and residents, in addition to working with colleagues to develop clinical pharmacy services in chronic disease areas. Our team put into play the lesson I learned from early life in the community pharmacy—always work hard. This, coupled with a continued focus on the patients served and a collaborative team approach, provided a rewarding pharmacy practice and excellent learning environment for students and residents.

Service has always been important to our profession. Pharmacists are often key leaders in service in their communities, which contributes to the high regard citizens hold of our profession. It is through professional service that courageous pharmacy leaders have challenged the status quo and moved our profession forward. I had the opportunity to become involved in state professional organizations and to serve in elected offices fairly early in my career. This experience, particularly as President of the Mississippi Pharmacists Association (MPhA), afforded me the opportunity to learn more about federal and state laws governing pharmacy practice and to demonstrate the importance of advocacy.

I had the opportunity at a state level to represent pharmacy in public health forums, such as a Governor's Task Force, and to interact with healthcare agencies, such as the Division of Medicaid. In these elected positions, I traveled to Washington, DC, to interact with congressional members and staff through formal pharmacy legislative activities, which heightened my interest in the world of advocacy.

A number of years ago, our University administration established a health policy fellowship with U.S. Senator Thad Cochran in his Washington office. This fellowship initially targeted graduate-level students or residents, the first being pharmacy colleague Dr. Blake Thompson, who paved the way for many others. The fellowship evolved to target individuals who were more established in their career and had experience in healthcare. Soon after my time as President of MPhA, I received an invitation to serve as the Health Policy Fellow for Senator Cochran. Although I like to think of myself as a planner, especially for the small things such as a to-do list and upcoming travel, I have never been one to have absolute next steps and strict timelines with regard to my professional career. I believe in a greater plan, and things happen just as they should and in the right time, so I keep an open mind to new options and seize opportunities as they arise.

When I received the invitation to participate in the fellow program, I was a faculty member with the UM School of Pharmacy, content with my career and its trajectory. I had patients, students, and residents who made each day fulfilling with new challenges, opportunities to learn, and rewarding interactions. From a personal perspective, I had recently married, moved into a new home, and did not have plans to relocate. But opportunity knocked, and I felt compelled to explore it. This exploration led to 2 years in Washington, DC, as Health Policy Advisor to U.S. Senator Thad Cochran.

The transition to this new role was somewhat surreal, stepping into an environment far outside my comfort zone of academic pharmacy. My world changed from direct patient care and teaching to congressional hearings and constituent visits, from scholarly manuscripts to briefing memos, and from neatly pressed lab coats to professional suits. I had the opportunity to learn in depth about pharmacy policy issues. My first day in the office was January 1, 2006, the day the Medicare Modernization Act was implemented. This legislation directly impacted community pharmacy practice, and my experience in this area was helpful as I fielded calls from pharmacist constituents and worked with Senate colleagues to address these unforeseen implications for our profession.

While in Senator Cochran's office, I was fortunate to meet many people in healthcare from my home state, professional associations, and federal agencies.

This network I established of healthcare colleagues has remained strong and been very helpful in all endeavors. I learned intricate details of the legislative process, such as how to draft new legislation and mechanisms to incorporate changes to proposals. Senator Cochran was Chair of the Appropriations Committee at that time, and significant work was focused on funding for the Department of Health and Human Services, National Institutes of Health, U.S. Food and Drug Administration, and other agencies. In the second year, my Policy Advisor responsibilities expanded to include appropriations for the Department of Housing and Urban Development (just after Hurricane Katrina devastated the Gulf Coast), the Department of Labor, and work on certain economic development projects for our state.

This incredible experience afforded me the opportunity to learn a great deal about policy, politics, healthcare, and pharmacy. I saw first-hand how policy at that level impacts day-to-day operations in almost every sector. Each day I met with individuals advocating for a specific issue, lobbyists with a full-time focus in an area, or constituents sharing personal experiences. From this, I learned the importance of advocacy at all levels, effective ways to present information and make requests, and how to be a resource in one's area of expertise or interest to staff members.

I also saw areas of my home state in a new light and understood challenges that different communities face and the strong assets we have in some regions. It was evident how chronic disease plagues much of Mississippi, specifically in our Mississippi Delta region; I learned about efforts underway to address this. My experience also provided a broad perspective for healthcare. As a pharmacist, I had been very focused on the specific issues related only to our profession and often times even more granular to those impacting a particular practice area. Stepping out of pharmacy and working in the broader healthcare arena helped me to better understand how pharmacy fits into that larger picture. It helped shape my vision for pharmacy and made me realize how each one of you can contribute toward improving healthcare in our nation. It helped me to dream big for our future.

We have had extraordinary leaders in pharmacy in our state and in our institution. At the end of my 2 years in Washington, I returned home to Mississippi to serve our School of Pharmacy as Associate Dean and Chair of Pharmacy Practice. With the support of Dean Barbara Wells and my predecessor, Dr. Joseph Byrd, and through work in Washington and our state, a vision of having transformative pharmacy services was provided for those areas with great need. In 2008, the School of Pharmacy implemented a community-based research program to provide access to comprehensive medication management services as part of healthcare teams in community pharmacies and provider clinics in the Mississippi Delta region. This program was structured to evaluate the impact of pharmacy services on patient outcomes, and results have been positive. The projects in this program contribute to our profession's effort to advance the practice of pharmacy. Working with federal agencies, specifically related to funding, has been helpful in my current role as we established an infrastructure for the School of Pharmacy and are presently building our research enterprise.

From childhood through this point in my career, what I have learned from my role models and mentors has served me well. It is what I attempt to apply in my own life and what I share with you today—work hard, seize opportunities, and dream big.

Best,

Leigh Ann

Elisabeth (Liz) M. Simmons, PharmD, BCPS

Having One Foot in the Clinical Realm and One Foot in the Operational Realm

In reflecting on her career thus far, Liz offers advice such as build your village, it's ok *not* to know, you might fail, you should learn how to tell a story and teach others how to be storytellers, and you should not turn down unique opportunities. Liz practices clinically and is a leader demonstrating that your career doesn't have to be one dimensional.

Elisabeth (Liz) M. Simmons is currently Clinical Pharmacy Manager and postgraduate years (PGY) 1 and 2 Pediatrics Residency Director (RPD) at Children's National Medical Center. Previously, she was Clinical Pharmacy Manager and PGY2 Pediatrics RPD at the University of Chicago Medicine. She received her PharmD from the University of Illinois at Chicago. Liz completed pediatric specialty and pharmacy practice residencies at the Medical University of South Carolina.

Liz's advice is: **Look for a boss who will serve as your coach, mentor, and finally your sponsor. Have open discussions about your needs and expectations, and don't be afraid to occasionally ask for what you need as a professional.**

Dear Young Pharmacist,

Welcome to the profession of pharmacy—it's a great place to be! As a profession, we have never been more perfectly poised and positioned to become a true primary care provider for all of our patients. Drug and healthcare costs are on the rise, and insurance companies have taken note, demanding not just provision of services but also *quality* provision of services. Additionally, safety continues to be a huge issue, with major steps needed to ensure that we do no harm. All pharmacists must work toward incorporating best practices into their day-to-day practice at the frontline and also for all the patients we serve.

As I reflect back on the almost 10 years I have spent as a clinical practitioner and now clinical leader, I have learned a lot of lessons along the way. The following are a few of the highlights.

Build your village. As a clinician leader, I wear a lot of hats—clinician, boss, RPD, scheduler, troubleshooter, party planner, mentor, and mentee. You name it; I've tried the hat on for a minute. One of the best ways to be successful when wearing multiple hats is to make sure that you have a solid team of practitioners and leaders you can trust to help you build and grow your vision. As you build your practice, this will include not only your co-workers but all members of a patient care services team. We can no longer afford to practice in professional silos. As you take on your frontline leadership roles, you'll want to build important connections, knowing which nursing manager is your go-to for developing quality services on your unit, who on the pharmacy team can help you solve an electronic medical administration record (eMAR) problem, and how to best implement a new clinical service. Additionally, you must build trusting relationships not only with your co-workers but with those to whom you report.

Your village is your sounding board, and those people will always have your back. Sometimes they will challenge you, but that is important to produce the best possible outcome for patient care. Use your village to have open conversations and uninhibited brainstorming sessions. Always keep the patient at the heart of what you do, knowing that it will always produce the best decision.

It's OK to not know. As pharmacists, we are hard-wired to want to provide the quickest, most accurate answer while frequently working independently. As you grow as a leader, you will find that there is not one correct way to solve a problem, and that engaging others in decision-making will almost always result in a better solution. Use the village that you've built to group problem solve, hold uninhibited brainstorming sessions, and allow for some conflict. Remember you may not know the best way to get from A to B, but your village can help you get there.

Just as I did not always know every answer to a specific clinical question off-hand, I do not always know the answer to every leadership dilemma. What I *do* promise is that in pulling together we can work through it. For a successful relationship, we must be honest with each other, enabling us to build a stronger path moving forward. You should have at least one person in your village who you can drop your guard around—someone you feel completely comfortable with and trust to bounce ideas off of. This person will help you when you need someone to confirm that you're doing the right thing, or that you're forging the correct path moving forward. It is infinitely easier to make difficult, unknown decisions when you have someone who can help you vet your thought process, and who won't hold your decisions against you when you occasionally take a misstep. Speaking of missteps, my next section is a great seque.

Sometimes, you're going to fail. As young RPDs, we had the opportunity to change clinical practice through developing an in-house pharmacy resident on-call model. Our vision was to provide a pharmacist at bedside 24/7 to ensure safe and effective care including code coverage, pharmacokinetic dosing, and drug information. As we were developing our program, we did not fully understand the impact that updated duty hour expectations were about to have on our planning—essentially not allowing our PGY1 residents to spend 24 hours in the hospital anymore. We took the lead from our medical resident colleagues, developing a "night float" model. We went from one resident providing 24 hours of continuous coverage, to occasionally three residents providing coverage in a 24-hour period. With this change in coverage, our number of near-miss pharmacy events greatly increased, likely due to ineffective and incomplete pass-off between shifts. We had failed as a group. Our residents were exhausted, not clinically present on rotation, and patient care was far from ideal. There had to be a better way.

Thankfully, we had a Director who encouraged innovative practice models and understood that failure was occasionally needed to advance practice. As a group, we came together to work through a solution—adherence to duty hours and fewer pass-offs throughout the day. We took what was initially a failure and used the experience to build a better model—something that would not have occurred without allowing failure. A good boss will allow you to fail but support you in moving forward with a better solution.

Learn how to tell a story and teach others how to be storytellers. Pharmacists are doers by nature. We excel at completing tasks that are assigned to us but frequently fail at promoting the outcomes. We tend to complete one task and then move on to the next. As a profession, we are primed and ready to be at the forefront of patient care, but it's not going to happen unless we spread the word about the safe, high-quality care we provide. Learn how and when to tell a story. Highlight your success in both formal and informal ways. Recognize the good work of others. Develop your own annual operating plan and share it with your boss. Work with your colleagues to develop a pharmacy annual report to highlight your successes. Participate in interdisciplinary committees and quality events. Share your stories with colleagues at local and national meetings. We all have something to learn from each other as we work to enhance patient care.

Try not to turn down unique opportunities. It's an exciting time in pharmacy. Every opportunity that is presented to you is an opportunity to grow, even if you think it is outside of your scope as a practitioner. Never discount an opportunity because you think that it's not your job or that it's not important to your immediate task at hand. By volunteering to help build our large volume infusion library, I formed lasting relationships with nursing managers and educators across the medical center. This has led to collaborative projects beyond what we ever thought was possible including instituting quiet hours for patients, delivering medications to the bedside, and making sure that patients who go home are not readmitted for medication-related issues.

Look for a boss who will serve as your coach, mentor, and finally your sponsor as you advance your clinical practice and develop as a leader. Have open discussions about your needs and expectations, and don't be afraid to occasionally ask for what you need as a professional. Your professional needs will change over time as you develop as a practitioner. There will be times when you need a coach to help you navigate the maze that is the healthcare arena. But as you develop professionally, there will be times when you only need someone to have your back. Be clear in your expectations and needs, and you will be rewarded with a fruitful career.

As a clinical leader, I frequently have one foot in the clinical realm and one foot in the operational realm. I've found that understanding—and living—both sides is vital to advancing practice. I frequently take the opportunity to change a practice based on something that happened with an individual patient (e.g., a medication error). If it can happen once, it can happen again. Being a leader means you can shape practice not just for one patient, but for all patients. Future endeavors in the profession will not be possible unless everyone takes a leadership role. Seek out opportunities to grow as a professional and always remember your personal development needs. Be a frontline leader even if it is not formally required of you. You are the pharmacist who best understands your patients' needs, and you are responsible for making sure that they receive safe and effective care.

Best wishes in all of your career endeavors, and always remember to keep patients at the center of everything you do.

Liz

Kelly M. Smith, PharmD, FASHP, FCCP

Being Successful as a Tenure Track Faculty Member

Kelly traces her career development and shares the lessons she has learned along the way, including her initial reluctance to take a tenure track faculty position because she did not feel prepared.

Kelly M. Smith is currently Associate Dean, Academic and Student Affairs, and Professor, Pharmacy Practice and Science, University of Kentucky, College of Pharmacy. She completed a previous term as Interim Dean. Kelly has chaired the ASHP Section of Clinical Specialists and Scientists and served on the ASHP Board of Directors. She received her PharmD/BS in Pharmacy from the University of Georgia and completed a specialized residency in drug information practice at the University Medical Center (now UF Health Jacksonville).

Kelly's advice is: *Rather than taking on challenges and opportunities as they come, make things happen for yourself. Remember that every professional interaction is an opportunity to make an impression on someone.*

Dear Young Pharmacist,

I have always enjoyed learning, yet I never dreamed that I would help others learn how to be pharmacists. Nor did I realize the lessons I would continue to learn throughout my career. After graduating from the University of Georgia, I entered a drug information residency at what is now UF Health Jacksonville in Jacksonville, Florida. Because I am a perfectionist, it was a challenge to learn how to manage multiple priorities to yield the best collective outcome. The responsibilities required contributing heavily to precepting students, and my resident colleagues forced me to quickly hone my ability to guide, collaborate, and advise others. I then became a Drug Information Specialist at the University of Kentucky (UK). I learned that the introvert in me enjoyed facilitating the success of others, from shaping a physician's approach to caring for a complex patient, to developing a student's ability to critically analyze the literature, to connecting a resident seeking employment with a colleague.

As I began guest teaching at the UK College of Pharmacy, I realized that I enjoyed helping others learn. Dr. Bob Rapp, a world-renowned clinical pharmacist and my department Chair, challenged me to pursue a tenure track faculty position. Out of naïveté, lack of self-reflection, and lack of confidence, I did not feel prepared to take on the research expectations of a tenure track faculty position so I became an Adjunct Assistant Professor. As I explored my identity as a Clinician/Instructor, I became more engaged with the pharmacy residency program. Soon, the Director of Pharmacy asked me to lead the pharmacy practice residency upon his departure from the university. This was something I had not anticipated. This storied residency program created by Paul Parker, a pioneer of pharmacy (and former ASHP President), had always been led by a Director of Pharmacy. Only 4 years out of my own residency, I was the Director of the UK program, working with preceptors who were world-renowned clinical experts that trained emerging leaders of the profession.

Just months into my tenure, our program underwent a fortuitous event—an ASHP residency accreditation survey. I collaborated with our preceptors and residents to push the program to greater heights based on the results of the accreditation process. Great things emerged, including the creation of the nation's first residency teaching certificate program and a more intentional approach to our well-established resident on-call program. I learned that our experiences could benefit residency programs across the country; postgraduate training innovations became a topic of research for me.

My confidence in teaching, contributing to the professional literature, and leading groups of colleagues was growing. I was promoted from the entry-level position of Assistant Professor to Associate Professor. I contributed to committees within the Kentucky Society of Health-System Pharmacists and other pharmacy organizations, including the American College of Clinical Pharmacy (ACCP) and the University Health-System Consortium Pharmacy Council. It quickly dawned on me that the more opportunities I had to bring my ideas for a program, department, college, or organization to fruition, the more I enjoyed leadership—a role I previously thought required the personality of an extrovert.

I began seeking opportunities to lead in the drug information practice setting. Although some positions were outside of UK, I valued its blend of practice, teaching, scholarship, leadership, and professional development. Soon, my Drug

Information Center Director announced that she was leaving, and things were seemingly falling into place for me. However, the Director's role was associated with a tenure track faculty position, which would require me to perform more as a researcher. My previous conversation with Bob Rapp came back to haunt me— why not be in a tenure track? The center's Director gave me the confidence that I was capable of handling the research expectations.

In a tenure track faculty position, you must cultivate a reputation as a leader and expert in a particular area of focus. That was initially challenging for me, as I viewed myself as a generalist, not focused on a particular disease state or population. After deliberating, I elected to focus on drug information advances in addition to sharing innovations in postgraduate training. I had a drug information leadership role in ACCP, and the doorway for ASHP leadership was about to open as I was invited to join the Commission on Credentialing (COC), the group that sets standards for and accredits residency programs. The invitation took me aback, as I had revered past COC members throughout my career. Although I did not consider myself to be in their league, it was an invitation I could not refuse. I do not know how I was identified to serve in that role, but it was likely a combination of interactions with accreditation surveyors, scholarly work, and my professional network. More importantly, I learned that every professional interaction is an opportunity to make an impression on someone.

My time on the COC was invaluable. I learned about the responsibility one accepts when serving as chair of a standards-setting committee, how to conduct a meeting of colleagues who are focused on critical professional issues, and how to make difficult and unpopular decisions. As an accreditation surveyor, I learned how to encourage my national colleagues to innovate within their residencies while gaining ideas that I would later incorporate into the program I directed.

Next, I learned the risks and rewards of reinventing myself. I no longer found the daily operations of a drug information center fulfilling, and the need for the center lessened as more practitioners satisfied their information needs through web-based resources. I was encouraged to seek professional leadership opportunities (e.g., Pharmacy Director, Assistant Dean). After much soul-searching, the Director of Pharmacy supported my move away from traditional drug information practice to medication-use policy. Other colleagues criticized the move, especially given UK's role in the development of drug information as a pharmacy specialty. Yet, I saw this as a time to determine where I truly wished to take my career. My COC term was concluding, and I feared a void in my professional career without continued involvement in ASHP. Once again, a call from a colleague came, encouraging me to pursue election as Chair of ASHP's Section of Clinical Specialists and Scientists.

As the next chapter in my ASHP leadership journey unfolded, I learned the importance of being true to myself and trusting my intuition. As I entered my tenth year as Residency Program Director, the role was becoming monotonous so I relinquished it. I turned my focus to facilitating the growth of residency programs across Kentucky, and the Kentucky Pharmacy Residency Network was born. The world of academic leadership suddenly opened for me. I participated in the American Association of Colleges of Pharmacy Academic Leadership Fellows Program to explore careers in academic administration. The program forced me to reflect on my strengths, identify gaps in my knowledge base, and reflect on my career. Until then, I had been taking on challenges and opportunities as they came my way, but I learned that I had to make things happen, not let them happen. I determined that an immersion in academia was right for me, although leaving my role in the patient care setting was difficult.

My Dean suggested that I would fit well in student affairs, with a plan to expand my leadership to the larger academic affairs role in several years. This resonated with me—it would be like serving as a Residency Program Director, but for many more trainees (students), and collaborating with more preceptors (faculty). I became Assistant Dean of Student Affairs. Soon I realized that succession planning is critical. Within a year, the Associate Dean of Academic Affairs stepped down unexpectedly, thus accelerating my leadership plan. As Associate Dean of Academic and Student Affairs, I would sacrifice my career advancement for what was best for the college and its constituents, meaning that my promotion to full Professor would be delayed several years.

Although my ASHP Section of Clinical Specialists and Scientists' leadership term had concluded, I did not feel my ASHP leadership journey had concluded. I had served the state affiliate in a variety of roles and ASHP as a Commission Chair, a member of a council (Therapeutics), and a Chair of a section. The next logical step was to pursue election to the Board of Directors, but that required a different level of commitment. At that time, I was working for a new Dean, so my time was limited. I continued to serve as time would permit. I applied twice for membership on ASHP councils but was not appointed. I perceived that as rejection, and it was difficult to accept. In retrospect, it taught me patience and perseverance.

Within a few years, I was positioned to dedicate sufficient time as an ASHP Board member, and I had the Dean's support, so I applied to the Committee on Nominations. As my candidacy was considered, I learned that not only were my contributions to the profession and the organization important, but the impressions I made on other leaders were also valued. Years earlier, the ASHP Past President encouraged me to see myself as the eventual Chair of the COC, which would be a springboard for future ASHP leadership roles. At the time, I was flattered, but doubted that I had the credentials or personality. I admittedly (and naively) viewed greater leadership roles within ASHP to be reserved for people with big titles, like directors of pharmacy. Now, I was one of four pharmacists slated for Director and was eventually elected. That experience taught me that timing is important, as I may not have been elected or even slated had I pursued the position years earlier. I also learned not to take the process of seeking appointment or election to leadership roles personally, regardless of the outcome.

Back at UK, I was finally promoted to full Professor. The delay in that promotion was well worth it, as I enjoyed my leadership role. The Dean announced that he was promoted to Provost. While I was happy for him, I wondered what would be next for me. Although I was a tenured Professor, I served as a member of the Dean's leadership team, which meant I served at the pleasure of a Dean who was leaving. Instead, I should have focused on who would be named Interim Dean, as I was requested to do just that. I was unprepared for such an offer, and I expressed concerns about my ability to meet the Provost's expectations. The old Kelly was coming out again, uncertain of her abilities to step up and lead, while those around her saw someone capable of leading. However, the Provost and now former Dean had been an important mentor, and I trusted his confidence in me. With his support and that of my leadership colleagues, I accepted the role. I was reminded of the lessons I learned throughout my professional journey—trust the advice of mentors, be authentic in your interactions, lead according to your strengths, and be open to all that pharmacy has to offer.

So where am I now? I have learned that I want to be Dean one day. If I had lacked the courage to say "yes" to so many opportunities along my professional journey, I may never have had the good fortune to explore this next potential phase of my career. More importantly, I have learned that I cannot escape learning and, as a pharmacist, I should **#alwaysbelearning**.

May you **#alwaysbelearning**,

Kelly

Eric M. Tichy, PharmD, BCPS, FCCP, FAST

Keep Your Eyes Open and Seize Opportunities

Serendipitous opportunities mark Eric's career from taking an unfilled residency slot to creating the pharmacist's role on the transplant service that, at the time, was not "pharmacy friendly." These opportunities started with finding a purpose in clinical practice into now leading 35 clinical pharmacists; being recognized as a Fellow of the American College of Clinical Pharmacy and American Society of Transplantation; and serving as a contributing editor of *AJHP*.

Eric M. Tichy is currently Manager, Clinical Services, and Director, postgraduate year (PGY) 2 transplantation residency, Yale-New Haven Hospital. Previously, he was Senior Clinical Specialist, Solid Organ Transplant. Eric received his PharmD from the University of Connecticut and completed a pharmacy practice residency at Yale-New Haven Hospital.

Eric's advice is: ***Open opportunities for members of your pharmacy team and for mentees. By remaining positive, you can help them find valuable opportunities when they least expect it.***

Dear Young Pharmacist,

Growing up, my father often advised me to "keep your eyes open, because you might find something valuable when you least expect it." At the time, I thought he was referring to the possibility of finding loose change on the ground. However, as I have matured into a professional, that lesson has translated into the trick of recognizing a good thing when I see it no matter how odd or worthless it might initially appear, even if someone else just walked by and left it behind. Several times in my career, tremendous opportunities have serendipitously presented themselves. Executing them has resulted in a rewarding career. Those rewards include recognition as a Fellow of the American Society of Transplantation and the American College of Clinical Pharmacy; appointment as contributing editor of the *American Journal of Health-System Pharmacy*; and recognition as a Service Excellence Hero at Yale-New Haven Hospital.

The first of these key opportunities occurred during my last year of pharmacy school at the University of Connecticut. When I entered my P4 year, I lacked clear direction for my future career. However, I started my clerkship rotations with my eyes wide open. Although I had worked in both the community pharmacy setting and at a small hospital throughout pharmacy school, I had not done my homework on residency training. This lack of appreciation for the value of residency left me in a position where I did not attend the ASHP Midyear Clinical Meeting nor did I participate in the residency match. I did, however, apply for an entry-level pharmacist job at Yale-New Haven Hospital; when they were left with an unmatched residency spot, I was at least astute enough to accept the residency position instead of the staff position. The key factor to getting that residency spot was my demonstration of excellence in my clerkship while at Yale-New Haven, and that body of work made all the difference in creating the conditions for the next opportunity.

After completing my residency, I worked in the clinical float pool at Yale-New Haven. This gave me the opportunity to practice throughout the organization in multiple specialties including critical care, medicine, surgery, and even pediatrics. Three years later, Yale-New Haven made significant investments in the organ transplant service line, and the new Program Director—a surgeon—made hiring a dedicated transplant clinical pharmacist a high priority. Prior to this time, the transplant service was not considered "pharmacy friendly," and I was stunned to hear one of the transplant surgeons express on rounds in the surgical intensive care unit that he "did not see why a clinical pharmacist was needed."

Needless to say, there was little to no interest from the rest of our clinical pharmacy team in this position. In fact, I did not apply for the position when it first opened. Fortunately, at the time there were few transplant pharmacy residency programs; therefore, the leadership at Yale-New Haven was not successful in recruiting a candidate from outside the organization. Two of my mentors, Lori Lee, the Clinical Manager, and Lisa Stump, the Director of Pharmacy, helped me see the golden opportunity of the transplant pharmacist role. They committed to supporting my attendance at national conferences and site visits to other transplant programs; they saw that my purpose was to make Yale-New Haven a nationally recognized practice of excellence in transplant pharmacy. I now manage the transplant pharmacy clinical team that includes two abdominal organ transplant pharmacists, a heart transplant and advanced heart failure pharmacist, and a PGY2 resident.

Growing and leading the transplant pharmacy team also became one of the greatest personal development exercises in clinical leadership I could ever design. I moved from learning to lead myself to teaching others to lead themselves in my roles as Residency Program Director and Senior Clinical Specialist. I also learned how to influence the organization's service line leaders and to secure pharmacist resources. Moreover, this experience in transplantation has further led to national leadership roles as a founding member of the American Society of Transplantation's Pharmacist Community of Practice Executive Committee, co-authorship of a number of key position statements on transplant pharmacy practice, and speaking engagements at national meetings.

Jack Canfield, author of the *Chicken Soup for the Soul* series, noted in his book *The Success Principles* that "Once you have paid the price to establish yourself as an expert, a person of integrity who delivers high-quality results on time, you get to reap the benefits of that for the rest of your life." My journey in developing expertise in transplantation and taking leadership roles in shaping the growth of the transplant pharmacy discipline has empirically proven the profound truth of his statement. Some of my most interesting life stories have occurred as a transplant pharmacist, and my expertise in immunology led to another unexpected opportunity.

A favorite story from my time as a transplant pharmacist occurred when our Heart Transplant Surgery Chief invited me to fly on a jet with the heart transplant team to recover an organ in Nashville for one of our patients. Notably, our patient was core positive for hepatitis B. During one of our weekly transplant evaluation meetings a few weeks prior, we discussed an organ offer that we had turned down due to the donor's serologic status of hepatitis B core positive. I knew from my liver transplant experience that we could manage the core positivity pharmacologically, so I suggested that we accept the organ. The following week, I researched the subject and presented my findings to the committee. Although many programs currently do not use hepatitis B core positive hearts, there are many successful reports in the literature. Given the severe organ shortage in our region, we ultimately determined it was worth considering in specific cases. This all culminated a month later with me flying with the transplant team to recover the heart in Nashville. I watched the entire transplant surgery and helped determine the full medication regimen, including immunosuppression and hepatitis B prophylaxis. Almost 8 years later, that patient is still alive and well.

Another unexpected opportunity arose in 2009 when Lee Ann Miller, Associate Director of Drug Use Policy, and Lisa Stump assigned me to manage immunoglobulin utilization for Yale-New Haven. Immunoglobulin is consistently a top 5 drug expenditure in our organization as it is in many health systems across the

United States. Given my expertise in immunology, experience with using the products in transplantation, focus on getting things done, and commitment to excellence, there was little doubt that I could make an impact on immunoglobulin utilization. In subsequent years, I implemented multiple interventions (e.g., adjusted-body weight dosing in overweight patients, dose rounding), eliminated pooling of doses, revised treatment protocols, converted formulary products, moved infusions into the ambulatory setting, and negotiated better pricing. These initiatives saved our health system multiple millions of dollars per year and helped me launch the concept of immunoglobulin, otherwise known as antibody stewardship.

Since 2009, I have given over 70 presentations in 25 states, written online continuing education programs, and published peer-reviewed journal articles on the concept of the pharmacist as the antibody steward. My work with immunoglobulin also helped introduce me to Jerry Siegel, who has been a gracious mentor and role model over the past 5 years. Jerry, now a retired Director of Pharmacy from Ohio State, was one of the pioneers of clinical pharmacy in the 1970s and 1980s. He demonstrated a pathway for clinical pharmacists as leaders in healthcare and is still the foremost authority on immunoglobulin management. Jerry and Rita Alloway, Professor of Surgery at the University of Cincinnati and pioneer of transplant pharmacy, have also helped me see the next phase of my career because a clinical leader should focus more on helping others climb the mountain. I now find my greatest satisfaction in creating opportunities for members of my pharmacy team and for my mentees, which include many of the alumni from the transplant pharmacy residency.

Although I share the truth that transplant pharmacy is simply nirvana for the ambitious clinical pharmacist and can lead to tremendous career growth, I have also observed that many of the principles of a great career in transplantation and immunology can translate into other clinical pharmacy disciplines and even translate to healthcare leadership in general. In my current role as a Manager of Clinical Pharmacy Services, I am now teaching my entire team of 35 clinical pharmacists how to get things done, the benefits of being a lifelong learner, and how remaining positive can help them find valuable opportunities when they least expect it. I am confident these future leaders will soon be recognized as fellows of whichever organizations they choose to commit their time and passion. I also look forward to a future where the current generation of clinical pharmacy leaders emerges to take an even larger number of seats in executive levels of healthcare leadership.

Regards,

Eric

Jacob J. Tillmann, PharmD, BCPS

Conducting Successful Residencies

Jacob shares how he has refined, along with his Residency Program Directors, the residency process for postgraduate year (PGY) 1 and several PGY2 programs for which he has responsibility. His responsibilities include the recruiting, interviewing, and selection processes. He offers advice on mentoring and coaching residents, including those areas where he derives the most satisfaction.

Jacob J. Tillmann is currently the Pharmacy Residency Program Coordinator, North Florida/South Georgia Veterans Health System. Previously he was a Clinical Pharmacy Specialist. Jacob received his PharmD from Drake University and completed a geriatric specialty residency at the Gainesville VA Medical Center.

Jacob's advice is: **Find residents that fit your program. It will certainly help make your program and the residents who complete it more likely to be successful. Remember to take time away from your residency (or career) and do whatever recharges you. When you return the next day or next week, you are in the best possible mindset.**

Dear Young Pharmacist,

In early 2009, I was given the opportunity to take on a newly created position at the North Florida/South Georgia Veterans Health System in Gainesville, Florida. I became the pharmacy's Residency Program Coordinator, a position that developed as a result of the expansion of our residency programs—to include 18 PGY1 residents, two PGY2 residents, and a pharmacy fellow—and necessitated improved coordination for more trainees. I had worked in both acute and ambulatory care in the 6 years since completing my residency as well as completing an interdisciplinary, interfacility leadership development program within the Department of Veterans Affairs in preparation for taking on leadership roles as my career progressed.

Being a Residency Director is something that fit in well with my personal and professional goals. It allowed me to gain exposure to a leadership role while also allowing me to expand on my love of education. Because education is an important family value, I am passionate about training the next generation of pharmacists as well as incorporating training and education into my everyday practice. I also realized that by moving into this administrative role, I was able to impact more patients than I could in my day-to-day clinical practice. I might see 10-20 patients per day in my practice; but as Residency Coordinator, I help shape the practice of more than 20 residents each year that will then use the skills they learn in their clinical practices after completion of the residency.

For me, the position of Residency Coordinator comes with tremendous gratitude from residents throughout the year and especially at the end of the year. By far, the best part of my job is having residents tell me that they got the jobs they wanted, the location they wanted, or ideally both. There are also many thankless portions of the job. When I stepped into this role, I didn't fully realize what happens behind the scenes of a residency program to make it appear to flow smoothly—reviewing applications, conducting interviews, scheduling residents in learning experiences, attending meetings, developing preceptors, and preparing accreditation surveys and responses to the quality assurance reviews of the program. The list goes on, with a never-ending to-do list to make that next improvement (which is part of the perfectionism that we as pharmacists tend to exhibit).

When I started in this position, I talked with our current Residency Directors to determine how I could best assist them with their residents and how I could help with the transition of the residency class that had already been selected for the coming year. I talked with residents about how I could best support them and questioned my colleagues from around the VA about how they managed their programs. Utilizing the wealth of knowledge and experience of others allowed me to make better decisions about altering the program in a smarter way than trial and error and also reduced time spent on developing ideas. Never stop asking questions. You need to remember that others in your network or organization have experiences worth sharing, and you can learn from them. I realized some colleagues expanded the quality of residency programs in very unique ways; the more I talked to people around me, the more I appreciated that there will always be an opportunity to share ideas and continue to enhance my program.

Because of my experiences and discussions, the residency program here has continued to evolve over the 7 years that I have been in my position. We have reduced the number of PGY1 residents but increased our number of PGY2 residents and programs, which certainly has its advantages. But it also brings new challenges. Although it was always important to have the residents who best fit the program, now with five different PGY2 programs in our facility, selecting those residents became an increasingly important part of my job as the PGY1 Director. I have spent the most time on developing and maintaining this process because of the importance of getting the best people in the right positions.

After more than 7 years and reading more than 500 applications, I have developed the ability to read an application and, with a fair amount of confidence, determine how that candidate will fit into our residency program. With some minor adjustments each year to my scoring rubric, I feel that I have been able to objectively measure something *subjective*—the "feel" of an application and the "fit" of the candidate for our program. The development of the rubric, which can help you attract the best candidates, can make or break your residency program. Developing and owning your process is essential so that you can objectively find the candidates who are the best fit for your program.

My interview process is also something that is exceptionally time-consuming for me and the preceptors. Because we conduct individual interviews with the candidates selected for onsite interviews, this process takes the majority of the month of February. Taking the time to review applications and interview the candidates is essential to ensure selection of the best residents for your facility. I personally spend 1½-2½ hours with each person. To me, the time spent in the interviews more than pays off because it provides an opportunity to find the best candidates for our program, and it saves time and potential headaches for the upcoming year.

With the increase in our PGY2 programs, identifying the best candidates for our residency program has changed over time. It seems intuitive, but finding the best PGY1 candidates to seed your PGY2 programs will save everyone a lot of time and energy in the future. In the past several years, we have early committed many of our PGY1 residents into our PGY2 programs as well as matched others who had not decided to apply by the early commit deadline or wanted to explore other programs during the match. The benefits to keeping PGY1 residents for our PGY2 programs are immense because they do not require as in depth of an orientation, can extend their clinical experiences, assist with orientation of co-residents, and come in as a known entity. For the most part, you don't need to worry about what their performance will be like during the year because you already know their capabilities.

When I began the journey into this new position, I had every intention of using it as a means to develop my leadership style and to transition into a Chief of Pharmacy position, eventually finding a way to be more involved nationally in VA pharmacy. Between being offered the Residency Coordinator position and starting in it, my 2-year-old son suddenly and unexpectedly passed away. In addition to being in a professional transition, my life outside of pharmacy suddenly was turned upside down. My wife was 36 weeks pregnant with our second child at the time. In a matter of 3 weeks, I went from a clinically practicing pharmacist with a 2-year-old son and a second child on the way to starting a new professional chapter, dealing with the grief of losing a child, and going through the sleep deprivation and joy of a newborn.

It certainly wasn't how I had hoped to start off in my new professional endeavors, but I think it also gave me a lot of perspective on life. This has become a focal point of how I interact with my residents, and I try to teach them about the importance of developing a work-life balance. I talk about it during interviews with candidates and during orientation. I regularly remind my residents that their time away from our facility is their time, and they need to use it to do whatever recharges them. When they come back the next day or week, then they are in the best possible mindset to learn because that is ultimately what they are here to do. Although residency is an intense year, the perception that you have to give up work-life balance to be a successful resident is a misconception. I try to make sure my residents realize the importance of balance.

A residency program, like any part of any organization, takes on the characteristics and personality of the person who leads it. There are many ways to develop, organize, and lead a residency program. As the Residency Program Director, you should take ownership of the program and ensure that it takes on your personality. Find residents who fit *your* program. It will certainly help make your program and the residents who complete it more likely to be successful.

Regards,

Jacob

Jennifer E. Tryon, PharmD, MS

Mentors—A Gift

Jennifer views mentors as one of the few gifts you can give yourself in your career that will result in a drastically enhanced professional path. She offers advice on finding a mentor, logistics to develop the relationship, ground rules to establish the relationship, and ways to enhance the mentoring. Her discussion is illustrated with specific examples from her experiences. Jennifer also encourages everyone to be a mentor as it is a two-way street where both individuals learn from each other.

Jennifer E. Tryon is currently Associate Vice President and Chief Pharmacy Officer, Wake Forest Baptist Health. Previously, she was the Executive Director of Pharmacy and Interim Chief Pharmacy Officer at the University of Chicago Medicine. Jennifer has served as a Director-at-Large and Chair for the ASHP Section of Pharmacy Practice Managers and Associate Faculty for the Pharmacy Leadership Academy. She completed her PharmD at the University of Iowa and her MS in Health System Pharmacy Administration at the University of Wisconsin. She completed a pharmacy practice residency and specialty residency in pharmacy administration at the University of Wisconsin Hospitals and Clinics.

Jennifer's advice is: **A strong mentor-mentee relationship will affect your career—possibly altering its path and pace by allowing you to build on the immense network and experience of your trusted and accomplished mentor.**

Dear Young Pharmacist,

What is the recipe for achieving a fulfilling and successful life? I have asked myself this question many times, wishing for a flowchart I could follow to ensure I achieve my dreams and find happiness in each day, year, and decade. On many occasions, friends and I have talked about life questions such as the right time to take the next step in one's career, or how to be both a good parent and a good pharmacy professional. I do not believe that there is one right way to ensure a successful life, but these kinds of questions are perfect to discuss and evaluate with a trusted mentor and friend.

There aren't many gifts you can give yourself in your career that will result in a drastically enhanced professional path. If you were provided with a jar of fairy dust and told you could use it to make one professional wish come true, what would you wish for? My one wish would be for every pharmacy professional to have a mentor. When I look back on my career, a few major decisions had a significant impact on my career path and trajectory, but none of them is as significant as the impact of my mentor. A strong mentor-mentee relationship has altered the path and pace of my career by allowing me to build on the immense network and experience of my trusted and accomplished supporter.

As I think about it now, my dad was my first mentor growing up. We lived in Europe where he was a school principal with the Department of Defense. After I finished my sports practice, I would meet him in his office and we would drive home together. In this one-on-one time, he would talk about what leadership lessons he had learned and encourage me to try new things such as giving back through community service, learning to play the piano, and making new friends (a necessity because we moved every few years). He always had a smile on his face, and perhaps that is why I am always smiling. I lost him when I was in college, and it left a void in my life.

Ten years ago, I wasn't sure how to choose and develop a relationship with a mentor; I thought the relationships usually happened organically or else it just wasn't meant to be. A mentor is someone who has done (or is doing) what you want to do, or is a person you look up to and can learn from. My advice to my younger self is to ensure you select your person and ask them to be your mentor. Develop a strong personal relationship with them by going to coffee, scheduling routine calls, and learning about each other or finding some other way to have a dialogue. The more you share about yourself, the more a mentor can understand your circumstances and can help you. I have talked with friends regarding their frustrations with poor mentor-mentee connections. This often happens when you are not communicating your needs, or your mentor does not have adequate time to dedicate to meet your needs. If that has happened to you, have a candid conversation with your mentor; if you do not see improvement, consider asking a different person.

I would recommend the following logistics as you develop the relationship. First, set up routine times to connect (by phone or some other way) and commit to them as a high priority. If you want the relationship to work, it requires some form of routine connection. Because my mentor and I lived in different parts of the country, we set up monthly calls that eventually evolved into weekly phone calls. The content of our discussions varied and included discussions about ourselves and our life philosophies. It included specific work challenges and guidance—especially how to position myself to be appointed or nominated for state and national professional organization leadership positions and how to be successful so opportunities for advancement would become available. Early in my career, my mentor boosted my professional confidence by helping me find opportunities to speak and publish professionally. Other significant guidance has been when and how to continue building my CV and enhancing my name recognition (e.g., becoming a Fellow of ASHP). Other guidance encouraged me to get out of my comfort zone and apply for an Executive Director of Pharmacy position even though it meant skipping a step in the career ladder.

Second, have a set of ground rules that serves as the basis for your discussions and relationship that you both commit to. The two ground rules I recommend are confidentiality and candidness. Your discussions should be held in confidence, and you should be free to discuss anything with each other or even ask questions that you think you should already know the answers to: Is it time to look for another position? What should I expect when I submit an article? Do I have to take all the reviewer's suggestions? What should I do when I am told I'm not qualified for a job that I've been doing for 6 months? What options do I have when I'm unsuccessful in dealing with a difficult person? How should I handle a political quagmire or sticky situation? When I am upset, I ask my mentor if I am overreacting to situations and people, or if there were other things I should have considered in a particular circumstance.

Finally, make time to evaluate your relationship together. This can be done quarterly or with any frequency; unless you can provide feedback to one another, you will not be able to improve the quality of the relationship.

The impact of good mentor selection can shape you as a professional. Your mentor can be a giant—someone you look up to who shares their experience to prevent you from making the same mistakes he or she did (so you can make smarter decisions) and who propels you forward by sharing their network through introductions at professional meetings. Mentors can sponsor you when opportunities arise such as membership on the ASHP Women in Pharmacy Leadership Steering Committee or help open doors for you such as co-editing a pharmacy leadership book or teaching in the Pharmacy Leadership Academy. They can talk with you about how to successfully navigate unfamiliar territory such as dealing with unfair criticism from other department members. They are your support in the best and worst of times.

From my personal experience, I can always depend on only a few individuals no matter what the situation—my mentor is highly ranked on this short list. I never feel alone when facing tough decisions because I have discussed the circumstance with her, and she fully supports me. This does not mean that you will not hear when you have "screwed up"; in fact, your mentor may be the first and only person who informs you of a mistake or a less than optimal approach. However, when this feedback is shared with you, it is clear he or she has your best intentions at heart and wants to see you be successful.

So, my best advice to every pharmacy professional who wants to live a full and successful life is to have a mentor who is a good fit for you. Be sure to nurture the relationship and revel in the closeness you develop with that person. A mentor is your "chosen family" and a person you will hold in the highest regard. It's the relationship that pays out with infinity-to-one odds, because what you gain from the experience is beyond value. Remember, the more you share of yourself and your experiences and the more vulnerable and raw you are with your emotions and their impact, the better your mentor will be equipped to assist you.

May you choose your mentor well, and may the relationship guide you every day of your life because the knowledge, friendship, and experience that you acquire is the special gift of the mentor-mentee relationship.

Be willing to mentor others yourself as it is a two-way street, and you will learn from them. They will also challenge you to keep growing. As a leader, I develop my students, residents, and staff through mentoring techniques. It is satisfying to see the people you work with grow, achieve a rewarding career, and make a significant impact on patient care.

Regards,

Jennifer

Aaron P. Webb,
PharmD, MS

Legacies Aren't a Burden,
But a Blessing

As the son of an influential pharmacy couple and a graduate of the prestigious University of Wisconsin Masters of Science program, Aaron is no stranger to legacies and "bigger-than-life" role models. When he was a student pharmacist at the University of North Carolina where his parents have strong connections, he realized that having powerful legacies carries high expectations. Rather than begrudging his legacy, Aaron chose to embrace it, leveraging a strong network to his professional advantage and viewing it as a challenge to achieve his own career success.

Aaron P. Webb received his PharmD at the University of North Carolina Eshelman College of Pharmacy and his MS in Pharmacy Administration at the University of Wisconsin. He completed a 2-year residency in hospital pharmacy administration at the University of Wisconsin Hospital & Clinics. He is currently Pharmacy Manager of Inpatient Pharmacy Operations at UWHealth and Clinical Instructor at the University of Wisconsin School of Pharmacy. Aaron is responsible for providing leadership and oversight for all aspects of the pharmacy operations in the main hospital. An active member of the Pharmacy Society of Wisconsin and ASHP, Aaron was appointed to the Board of Pharmacy Specialties Sterile Compounding Practice Analysis Taskforce.

Aaron's advice is: ***Develop a career vision, with the ultimate professional goal of ensuring a body of work that constitutes a legacy of your own.***

Dear Young Pharmacist,

As a young pharmacist, I received sage advice from a mentor to develop and maintain a continuous professional development (CPD) plan so that I would have a blueprint for how I wanted to reach my career goals. This mentor was clearly in a great position to offer such advice being an icon in pharmacy himself. He encouraged me to think about what I wanted my legacy to be as I developed my CPD plan. A CPD plan is important in managing your own development to better understand where you are in your career and where you want to be in the future. Part of this CPD plan was to develop a career vision, with the ultimate professional goal of ensuring a body of work that constitutes a legacy of my own. For me, that involved leaving my "imprint" on the people and organizations with whom I work throughout my career.

People who know me from my undergraduate days would say that this is like an orange tiger paw on the road that leads into the football stadium at Clemson University. I want to create a legacy that demonstrates a positive impact to those I interact with in my professional and personal life. When I was younger, the thought of a legacy was not very important to me. It still didn't seem important as I transitioned into the young professional phase of my life, and in some ways the thought of a legacy made me feel uncomfortable. Now I realize how fast life and career seems to fly past and how important it is to focus on your goals and legacy, especially early in your career. In fact, it should be the ultimate goal for most professionals to leave an organization and the people around them in better shape than when they arrived.

One of the very first steps I took was to reach out to mentors whose legacies I admired to figure out how their own paths evolved. They challenged me to think about what has made me successful to this point, both professionally and personally, and why a legacy is fundamental to my larger career vision. I believe part of the basis for my perspective is that legacies of many types have always been a part of my professional life because both of my parents are pharmacists with impactful careers. This has helped me in many ways, but it has also presented challenges.

The upside of my legacy is that from a young age I was exposed to many opportunities in pharmacy as well as a broad network of successful pharmacists. This vast network afforded me the opportunity to meet great leaders in our profession. It also made me aware that there were many career paths in pharmacy and that it was a great profession. I always knew someone who could help me learn more about various areas of pharmacy or make the right connections. My supportive parents knew and understood the trials of several years of school followed by 2 years of an administrative residency. The values they instilled in me and their support nurtured a foundation on which my preceptors and mentors could build.

The downside of my legacy is a combination of expectations and preconceptions, which have always made me uncomfortable and sometimes even made me push my legacy away. At times, I have avoided letting my family connections be known. However, it seems that everywhere I go in pharmacy I meet people who can share a personal story about me, such as my youth baseball career or great passion for Clemson football, which they've learned from a connection to my parents. It made certain aspects of my early career very difficult as I have immense pride in my own abilities and didn't want people to think I was given something that I didn't earn. The result was an increased pressure to be successful—to go beyond my already strong competitive drive.

I first learned of the power of a legacy and the importance of having personal connections when I entered Clemson University. A friend, like an older brother figure who was 2 years ahead of me in school, had joined a social fraternity and opened the door for me to join when I arrived. I desperately wanted to be a part of this fraternity because I had heard about the brotherhood that existed in these environments and needed support so far from home. This is where I first learned to utilize a legacy to explore a path that otherwise I would have never considered or potentially been afforded. I am truly thankful as I formed lifelong friendships and bonds through my experiences in the fraternity.

I became aware of the pressures of a pharmacy legacy when I entered pharmacy school at the University of North Carolina, where both of my parents had strong ties. However, what I didn't fully appreciate at the time was the significant legacy of the Eshelman School of Pharmacy itself and the expectations placed on graduates of the program.

Pressure continued into the second phase of my pharmacy career as I entered the administrative residency program at the University of Wisconsin. The Wisconsin legacy is well known for great leaders and a strong network, so the idea of motivating me to live up to that legacy at such an historic program was very intimidating. This is where I truly began to understand what a legacy was and should be. It is also when I first learned to accept and be more comfortable with my legacy. It is something that comes with pressure, but at the same time can be inspirational. It aids in the development of strong roots on which to grow, yet doesn't define how you grow or tell you what you need to grow. That is something you must find out for yourself as your career path evolves. It is important that you don't lose sight of your legacy that afforded you opportunities and why you must pay it forward like those before you. To me, it is how the legacy was built—creating a positive impact for others while ensuring that you make those who came before you proud as they watch you develop your own career path.

I have come to more fully appreciate that legacies aren't a burden, but a blessing. Legacies matter and have significant impact on your life. Having been part of strong legacies, I now embrace them and try to take from each of them the parts that will make me a stronger professional. Hopefully, this will help me establish my *own* legacy. Finally, I have become comfortable with my legacy and know that I can control how I feel about it. I am thankful for all the benefits and challenges that go with it. It has helped make me who I am at this stage in my career and will continue to be a part of who I am.

A meaningful legacy will always be an essential element of my CPD plan. With continued good fortune and hard work, hopefully the organizations and people that I work with will be able to say the same thing about me in the future. I will remain committed to ensuring those who come behind me and who I have the opportunity to mentor will start off their career thinking about their own legacy. I will encourage them to have an appreciation for why legacies matter and advise them to have it as a goal in their CPD plan.

Regards,

Aaron

David E. Zimmerman, PharmD, BCPS

Integrating a Clinical Practice and Academic Career

David talks about his career decision points and shares his experiences establishing an emergency department clinical practice and meeting the challenges of academic scholarship so he wouldn't fall victim to the "publish or perish" peril. David and a co-editor developed and submitted a book proposal, which involved seeking and collaborating with contributing authors, and then ensured it was published. Needless to say his teaching, precepting, and scholarly activities sometimes demanded working on weekends; however, "he would do it over in a heartbeat."

David E. Zimmerman is currently Assistant Professor of Pharmacy, Mylan School of Pharmacy at Duquesne University, and Emergency Medicine Clinical Pharmacist at UPMC-Mercy Hospital. He received his PharmD from the Philadelphia College of Pharmacy, the University of the Sciences. David completed a postgraduate year (PGY) 1 residency at The Johns Hopkins Hospital and a PGY2 emergency medicine residency at Maimonides Medical Center.

David advises: *Always plan for the future. It could be a 3-, 5-, 10-, or 25-year plan and should include both your career and personal goals to ensure your life is balanced. It is perfectly ok if these goals change as you progress.*

Dear Young Pharmacist,

Lesson #1: Choose whichever inspirational phrase or quote that you like and repeat it when you are faced with some sort of adversity. Some common examples include "Ask not what your country can do for you, ask what you can do for your country"–President John F. Kennedy, "You miss 100% of the shots that you do not take"–Wayne Gretzky, and so on. I personally like *carpe diem*, a Latin phrase for "seize the day." This is a phrase made famous to me from the movie Dead

Poets Society. It was not until after Robin Williams passed away (the great actor in Aladdin, Mrs. Doubtfire, Good Will Hunting) that I saw the movie for the first time and ever since have latched onto that phrase. Ah, the good ole days.

I grew up in Lancaster, Pennsylvania (no, I am not Amish but did have Amish neighbors) and worked at an independent pharmacy owned by my best friend's father in high school. This is where my interest in pharmacy began. In high school, chemistry and math were some of the subjects I enjoyed most so my parents said, "Why don't you become a chemical engineer?" So that's what I thought I might pursue, but the more I worked at the pharmacy, the more I became fascinated with how a little pill can have a multitude of beneficial (and adverse) effects on patients. My curiosity for how drugs impacted the human body sparked my interest to attend the Philadelphia College of Pharmacy (PCP). At first I thought about focusing on laboratory research, but in my second professional year I applied for a new internship program geared toward students interested in hospital pharmacy and residency at the Philadelphia VA Medical Center. I did not know much about hospital pharmacy but was interested in expanding my horizons, shifting into a more clinical direction. I decided why not. It does not hurt to apply and see what happens. *Seize the day...*

From the day I started there, I knew I wanted to follow this particular path. It was enlightening to see intravenous medications for the first time, the intricacies of how an inpatient pharmacy operated, and the pharmacists' roles on interdisciplinary rounding medical teams. Although I was already involved in several pharmacy organizations, I began to attend Student Societies of Health-System Pharmacy (SSHP) meetings and learned about residency opportunities for hospital pharmacists. Through discussions with PCP faculty members and mentors, my interest was solidified to be a clinical specialist. My broad interest of clinical, research, and precepting learners made residency the most appropriate track for me.

I went on to complete my PGY1 at The Johns Hopkins Hospital where I found my clinical passion—emergency medicine. It was in the emergency department (ED) where I felt my personal skills were best used. I enjoy the challenge of managing patients when very little information is known, sometimes not even knowing their names or past history. Most importantly, I loved interacting with patients, not just the critically ill heading to the intensive care units or medicine floor but also the ambulatory population that would be discharged from the ED. I felt that I could have a huge impact in all of these areas. So I went on to complete my PGY2 in emergency medicine at Maimonides Medical Center in Brooklyn, New York. Here I learned how to manage a very busy ED and interact with a diverse patient population. I also completed a teaching certificate program, which sparked my interest in precepting students and teaching in the classroom.

Following residency, I had another tough career decision to make. (By now I realized the days of making tough career decisions did not end with my PGY1 match selection as I originally thought.) Do I focus solely on my clinical career? Maybe go to an academic hospital so I could precept residents and students? Or should I go into academia and focus on research and teaching? I finally ventured on a path that encompasses these three aspects of clinical pharmacy, as a clinical tenure track position with the Mylan School of Pharmacy at Duquesne University. At the college, I am expected to excel not only with teaching in the classroom but also in scholarship and service. Before I could begin the scholarship component, I had to first establish a new practice site. I was challenged with showing what a pharmacist could do in the ED because they previously did not have clinical pharmacy services. This was not easy—not by a long shot. My approach was to help out in any way that I could, which included compounding intravenous medications for a nurse and grabbing an infusion pump, calling an outpatient pharmacy to get a medication history, or simply helping a patient onto a stretcher or getting them a blanket. Eventually the physicians, nurses, patient care technicians, respiratory therapists, social workers, and others saw my value and welcomed me onto the team and began to utilize my clinical pharmacy knowledge. This did not happen right away and at times was frustrating, but I realized that this learning curve was perfectly normal. It brought me to the realization that life may not always be as easy as my generation might think, which leads me to my second lesson.

Lesson #2: "*Never give up . . . never ever give up*" spoken by the late Jimmy Valvano at the 1993 ESPY awards. He was referring to his battle with cancer that would eventually claim his life, but I feel these words can hold true in many situations. I persevered, went to my practice site each day with a positive attitude, and worked on building relationships with co-workers and helping patients. Over time, things improved and my abilities were utilized more and more. I would be remiss, though, in not acknowledging that I was very fortunate to have a physician and nursing champion. Without these individuals pushing to get an ED pharmacist, I would have never had the opportunity that I did. Now I am fully integrated into the workflow and sit on several committees, providing education to nurses, emergency medicine prescribers, and even emergency medical service personnel. Balancing time between the ED and college remains a challenge. There were (and still are) days that I wish I could be in the ED and see patients in addition to my responsibilities as a faculty member. I would then remember, "*Never give up, never ever give up.*"

With my practice site established, I could move onto scholarship activities. Scholarship is a big component of academia, especially when in a tenure track position. I knew when I first started that I would have to start developing ideas/proposals and seek research collaborators so I would not fall victim to the "publish or perish" peril of academia. As it turns out, my first project landed in my lap during the first year at my practice site. During a monthly ED departmental meeting, I was asked about our current management of community-acquired pneumonia in patients discharged from the ED. I mentioned our increasing resistance rate of *S. pneumoniae* to macrolides warranting a second agent and volunteered to update the treatment protocol with our infectious disease pharmacists and physicians. From there, I had an interdisciplinary research proposal and an opportunity for students to data collect. This got the ball rolling with scholarship, poster presentations, and peer-reviewed manuscripts.

My next big step in scholarship was putting a book proposal together for the text *Demystifying Drug Dosing in Obese Patients*, with my colleague and good friend Brandon R. Shank, PharmD, BCOP. This project was his idea that started with a simple discussion. We then created a proposal, drafted a chapter, and worked with ASHP Special Publishing to present this proposed project. After the proposal was accepted, we had the simple task of writing and editing the book (sarcasm intended). The process was not easy, and we had to learn some of the steps as time went on. We first had to recruit authors, demonstrating the power of networking throughout your career; get contracts signed; establish and manage deadlines; edit; and provide feedback to authors. Fortunately, we had great support from the ASHP Publishing staff. All of this work was in addition to my teaching and precepting responsibilities. Needless to say I spent many weekends dedicated to this project, but I would do it over again in a heartbeat. There were times when I questioned if I could do it, but I thought back to Robert F. Kennedy quoting George Bernard Shaw: "Some men see things as they are and say, why; I dream of things that never were and say, why not." Why couldn't we write and publish this book?

I would not have had this opportunity without my friendship with Brandon and his discussion with an ASHP Acquisitions Editor at one of the Midyear Clinical Meetings following a presentation on how to publish; this brings me to my next lesson.

Lesson #3: *Network, network, and network some more.* Pharmacy is truly a small world. I was told this as a student and resident, and I tell students and residents this all the time. Whenever you attend any meeting—local, statewide, or national—use the opportunity to network and introduce yourself to others. You never know where these connections will take you. It could be a collaboration for a future project, maybe an invitation for a presentation or a job opportunity, or simply and most importantly, a friendship that can last a lifetime.

My last piece of advice comes from a discussion on career goals I attended during my residency. **Lesson #4: *Always plan for the future.*** These plans could be 3-, 5-, 10-, 25-year, or combinations thereof. It is essential to start planning for the future. Although the plans should be based on career goals, they should always include personal goals, as it is imperative to have a work-life balance so time is spent with family and friends. What is the purpose of life if you do not live it? Remember, it is perfectly okay if these goals change. Since going into academia, I have had several career (and personal) life goals change; there is nothing wrong with that. For example, I am now involved in training pharmacists from Italy and was invited to present at a national meeting in Italy. I would have never dreamed of this when I was a student or resident. No one can predict the future or the directions healthcare will go or the new avenues that will emerge in pharmacy. The more you are prepared for your career trajectory, the more successful you will be.

I hope my experiences and lessons will help you along your own journey. I will close where I began.

Now go. *Carpe diem…*

David